PILLARS
OF
MENTAL PERFORMANCE MASTERY

A STORY ABOUT MASTERING THE MENTAL GAME AND WINNING IN LIFE

BRIAN CAIN
MENTAL PERFORMANCE COACH

"A great story for anyone who aspires to be a master of mental performance."

Sean Haggerty
MPM Certified Coach
Former US Navy SEAL & US Navy SEAL Instructor
CEO, Protector Brewery

"A must read for anyone who is working to be their best. The strategies found in this book are many of the same ones that were a part of my journey in a 19-year Major League Baseball career."

Raúl Ibañez
19-Year Major League Baseball Career
300+ Home Runs, 2009 MLB All-Star

"For the past two days, Brian Cain's *10 Pillars of Mental Performance Mastery* was my best friend. I didn't go anywhere without it. I didn't want it to end! Lots of great ideas, quotes and insights. One of the most 'fun' books I have ever read!"

Dr. Rob Gilbert
Creator of the Success Hotline - (973) 743-4690

"A must read for professional athletes or anyone at the top of their profession."

Tom Murphy
Former UFC Fighter

"Engaging from start to finish!"

Clint Hurdle
Manager, Pittsburgh Pirates

"Make no mistake about it, this book is about you. It will speak directly to you no matter what industry you're in. The central character is merely the vehicle to deliver Brian Cain's powerful message to each and every one of us. Do yourself a favor. Don't just read this book – absorb it and own it."

John Brubaker
MPM Certified Coach
Award-Winning Author, Speaker and Coach

"Point blank one of the best books I've ever read. Where was this when I was playing?"

Eric Byrnes
MPM Certified Coach
Analyst, The MLB Network
10-Year MLB Career
World-Class Ultra-Endurance Athlete

"One of the most informational and inspirational books I have ever read. I love it."

Lyndsey Fry
2014 Team USA Women's Hockey Silver Medalist

"*Mental Performance Mastery* is a staple in our locker room. All of our players will read this book every year. Cain and his system of *Mental Performance Mastery* are an integral part of our program and are at the core of how we prepare our team mentally to give them the best chance for success as people, students and players."

Cliff Godwin
Head Baseball
East Carolina University

"*Mental Performance Mastery* is book that I will share with my team and staff every year. It's a great reminder of the fundamentals it takes to Win Every Day."

Steve Wojciechowski
Head Basketball Coach
Marquette University

"Brian Cain and *Mental Performance Mastery* were a critical piece of our run to an NCAA National Championship. We reference him and his teachings on a daily basis."

Lonni Alameda
Head Softball Coach
Florida State University
2018 NCAA National Champions

"Brian Cain has been a part of our program since 2009 and our student athletes use his teachings daily to compete both on the field and in the classroom. He was big part of us winning our first ever NCAA National Championship."

Andy Shay
Head Men's Lacrosse Coach
Yale University
2018 NCAA National Champions

"Brian Cain helped us better learn how to compete one pitch at a time. Our staff references much of what he shared with us even years after he has been with us in person."

Pat Casey
Head Baseball Coach
Oregon State University
2006, 2007, 2018 NCAA National Champions

"I want to thank you Brian for *Mental Performance Mastery*. This book and the strategies you share to grow yourself and those you lead in each of the pillars has changed my life for the better. I am a better teacher, coach, husband and father because of applying these strategies. Thank you."

Ethan Miller
MPM Certified Coach
High School Baseball Coach & Athletic Director

Brian Cain, MPM
Mental Performance Mastery Coach
Brian Cain Peak Performance, LLC

Mental Performance Mastery

©2019 by Brian Cain, MPM, CMAA, MS

All rights reserved. No part of this book may be reproduced, stored in a retrieval system, or transmitted in any form or by any means (electronic, mechanical, photocopying, recording, or by any information retrieval system, or otherwise) without the prior express written consent of the author and Peak Performance Publishing, except for the inclusion of brief quotations in critical articles or a review.

Printed in the United States of America
Edited by: Mary Lou Reynolds

INTRODUCTION

Matthew Simonds is a well-respected and highly sought-after business consultant who has reached a pivotal crossroads in his life. Spending 280 days a year on the road is taking its toll on his health and on the relationship with his wife and kids.

He's on his way home from consulting in Detroit to celebrate Thanksgiving and his wife's birthday with the family when his travel plans get interrupted unexpectedly and put him into a tailspin of negativity, doubt and frustration with his life.

Coach Kenny, a former Olympic athlete and current Mental Performance Mastery (MPM) Certified Coach, happens to be sitting next to Matthew Simonds on the plane and invites him to get his mind right, to get a checkup from the neck up, stop feeling sorry for himself, and start living a life by design by following his system for optimal living called *The 10 Pillars of Mental Performance Mastery*.

Coach Kenny and Matthew Simonds take you on a journey into the soul of a man, the challenges that we all face and the system of success that has helped create champions in sports, business and life.

Mental Performance Mastery is the system that has helped Coach Kenny and will serve Matthew Simonds in his pursuit of becoming more so that he can give more.

It's the same system that will serve you in your pursuit of becoming the best you that you've ever been so you can start living the optimal life that you envision and win more every day.

CHAPTER 1
YOU HAVE TO BE KIDDING ME

It was a typical Wednesday and I couldn't wait to get home. I had been on the road for 13 straight days and was so fired up to see my wife Erin, daughter Brina and son Michael. I knew that if I could just make it through this grind of a week, I would be home for Thanksgiving tomorrow and her birthday on Friday. If I could just get home, I would be able to invest the time into my family that I wanted to but had been unable to because of being too busy at work.

We were sitting on the tarmac about ready to go wheels up and get in the air when my worst nightmare in that moment came true.

"Ladies and gentlemen, this is your captain speaking. We are having some mechanical issues and are going to have to return to the terminal."

My heart sank. Another delay. As I sat there, I muttered to myself, probably louder than I should have, "You have to be kidding me."

The old man sitting next to me with a black hooded sweatshirt pulled over his head, who I thought was sleeping, opened his eyes, looked over at me and said, "I'm sorry. What did you say, son?"

"Oh, nothing. I was just talking to myself," I said, taken a bit back by the direct nature of his question.

"Well, I thought you were complaining that we were going back to the terminal," he said. "I'm just glad we didn't take off. The last thing you want is for the captain to diagnose a mechanical issue once you have taken off – then none of us are getting home. Better late and alive than never, I always say."

"That's a great point. I just wish I could get home on time once in my life," I said.

"Home? Home is where your feet are. And right now home is on this plane, so you might as well enjoy it 'cause from the looks of it, we are going to be here a while," the man said. "My name is Kenneth John Henry Johnson. My friends call me Coach Kenny. What's yours?"

"I am Matthew, Matthew Simonds," I said.
 "Well, Matthew Simonds, it's nice to meet you. I am on my way home too. I live in Paradise

Valley, Arizona. Was here in Detroit seeing some of my friends."

"Coach Kenny, did you say you live in Paradise Valley, Arizona? So do I! Small world," I said. "Did you say you were in Detroit visiting some of your friends?"

"Yes. I work as a Mental Performance Mastery (MPM) Coach and although the corporate professionals, coaches and athletes I am working with up here are my clients, I consider them my friends. I think of them like that so that I can be my best for them, I love them like I do my closest friends, it's how I show up my best for them," Coach Kenny said. "What brings you here, Matthew Simonds?"

"My job," I said with a sigh. "I work as a business consultant and I was up here seeing some clients and putting out some fires. Nothing too exciting actually."

"That's too bad that you don't find what you do to be exciting. You only get one chance at this game called life, and one of the keys to victory is to bring the juice because if your juiceful, you're useful and if you are juiceless, you're useless. I've found that the secret to being fulfilled in life and the best way to bring the juice is to live in SIN.

Now don't get all religious on me, Matthew. What I mean by SIN is to find the intersection of your Strengths, Interests and the world's Needs. If you want to be ultimately successful, you must find your interests so strong that you would pay to do it, find your strengths so good that you could be the best in the world, and find out what the world needs so much that they would pay you for your expertise.

I have found that intersection of my strengths, interests and the world's needs and I get to live there every day. When you do that, you will never work a day in your life. I use SIN as an acronym so that people will remember; there is a little shock value there – and I am all about shock value because it gets your point across quickly and today, people never feel like they have time so you have to strike quickly and deeply if you want to make a difference," Coach Kenny said.

"After the Olympics I went to work as a MPM Coach and have never worked a day in my life – I love it. I'd pay to do it. It keeps me up at night and kicks me out of bed in the morning just like training for the Olympics used to. Now, at 70, I can't move as well as I used to, but my mental performance mastery is better than ever."

I had no idea I was sitting next to an Olympic athlete. My wife was an Olympic Ice Hockey player and I had always been fascinated with the dedication and commitment that she made to her physical training and to building up her elite mindset.

"Coach Kenny, you still look like you should be competing," I said. He was in great shape for any age. For 70, he was an absolute specimen. "That's awesome that you were an Olympian. What sport did you do?"

"I did the decathlon. You know, the one where you do four runs, three jumps and three throws and you get crowned as the best athlete in the world if you win," he said. "Well, I never won a medal, but the lessons I learned in training and the lessons I learned since the Olympics have been worth more to me than any gold medal would have been. Don't get me wrong; I love to win. I just love to learn more.
You see, Matthew Simonds, in life there are winners and... what do you think? Winners and..."

"Losers," I said.

"NO!" He exclaimed with an energy and passion I had not seen in a long time. "There are winners and learners in life, and the biggest gold medals of them all go around the necks of those who learn the most. You are either learning or you are getting left behind. You are either learning and growing or you are staying the same and dying. And it looks like you have a whole lot of learning to do, Matthew Simonds. How much do you travel for work?"

"About 280 days a year," I replied.

"280 days a year on the road, and you are married with kids?" Coach Kenny asked as he leaned in to get closer. "You won't be married for long based on my experience if you keep it up. Proximity is power in any relationship and if you are on the road that much, it sounds like you are living to work instead of working to live.

If you want to be connected to people, you must make the time for them and you must share adversity together, whether that be raising the kids, working out or going through hardships together. Challenge and adversity brings us closer, as does time."

Coach Kenny was right. I was treading on thin ice. I had let myself go physically, I was weighing in at 240lbs, a far shot from the 190lbs I was at when I felt my best.

I had not been as present with Erin, Brina and Michael as I wanted to be, and I had not been home much at all. The money was good, but the lifestyle, the fast food last minute eating, the travel they were all slowly killing me.

I wondered how Coach Kenny could know so much about me so fast sitting here on the tarmac? Was this guy a wizard or was I really wearing my life on my sleeve that easily for people to see? I thought that if he could see it, so could my clients, and maybe that was part of why I had been underperforming lately.

When we got to the terminal, passengers started getting up and heading off the plane and back inside. As I took my phone out of my pocket to text Erin that I was delayed again, I sat there numb, taking to heart what Coach Kenny had said about winners and learners, about either growing or dying, about being juiceful, about living in SIN, about proximity being power, and living to work vs. working to live. I used to love what I did but recently it seemed like that love had turned into resentment, as my work was taking me away from my wife and kids. I was always reminded that you only get to see them grow up once.

As I finished sending a text to Erin, I looked up and he was gone. I was one of the last ones on the plane. I got up and started to walk back into the airport terminal, hoping that they would get the plane to fly – I just wanted to get home.

CHAPTER 2
THE NEXT FLIGHT

When I got to the top of the jet bridge and walked into the airport, the line at the Northeast Airlines ticket counter looked like a line of people waiting to get into a Metallica concert – it was packed with world-class people with world-class hair mostly dressed in black. My flight from Detroit to Arizona wasn't the only one that had been delayed.

Rather than wait in line to find out what was going to happen, I called the Northeast Airlines customer service center. After waiting for almost 20 minutes, an operator picked up the phone and said she had good news and bad news. The good news was that due to the mechanical issue with the plane, I had automatically been booked on the next available flight back to Arizona. The bad news was that flight wasn't until Saturday morning.

"Saturday morning," I said with a rage of frustration. "It's Wednesday, Thanksgiving is tomorrow, and my wife's birthday is on Friday. I have to get home today."

"I'm sorry, Mr. Simonds. This is a busy time of year for travelers, you know, and that flight on Saturday is our next available seat," said the agent. "I checked with our partner airlines and they don't have any available seats either. Now, my records show that they haven't officially canceled your original flight yet, so I'd stay by the gate and keep your fingers crossed."

I learned early on that crossing my fingers and hoping were not strategies that were going to get me anywhere. I just wasn't sure what to do.

Then I heard a familiar voice.

CHAPTER 3
THE VOICE

As I made my way to find a seat at our gate in hopes of a status update on our flight, I heard a familiar voice.

"Hey Matthew, Matthew Simonds. Over here, son."

As I looked to my left, there was Coach Kenny sitting at a table inside the airport Protector Brewery and Burger restaurant, a high-level burger chain that was taking over the country. He was sitting with a burger and a cream soda.

"Come on in, son. We are going to be here a while. Might as well take a load off and fuel the machine," he said.

I thought to myself, *What the heck. I'm going to be here a while. I might as well sit with the old man and have one of the burgers that's taking the world by storm just like Fortnite, on your plate vs. on your screen.*

I went in, sat down and ordered my favorite Protector Brewery and Burger selection – a 2/3 pound burger with Swiss cheese, mushrooms, grilled onions and avocados on a bun made of a glazed donut. I got myself a cream soda as well and took a deep breath as I sat back in my chair, wondering how I was going to get home.

"We can't control the airline, the plane, the pilot and a whole heck of a lot of other things, so we might as well enjoy what we can control, which is some great food," Coach Kenny said with a smile.

"Now if I remember right, Matthew Simonds, did you say you were on the road 280 days a year?"

"Yes, about 220 too many," I answered. "I set a goal a long time ago to reach a level of financial security by the time I was 40 in which I wanted to have my house paid off, a strong security cushion in savings, and enough in my investments where I could draw about $5K a month in interest and live off that so I could be home more and basically retire. It's been a lofty goal and one I have been relentlessly pursuing for years now. A lot of times I wonder if the cost of pursuing that goal is worth it?"

"Damn, son. That's a big goal for someone as young as you," Coach Kenny said. "But that's what life is all about, setting and getting big goals. Setting big goals is great, but they have to be the right goals or they become traps. Financial goals must be secondary to family goals or you won't have any family to set goals with. You also need to have telescope and microscope goals. Telescope goals that you can see off into the future, and then you must reverse engineer a process back to your microscope and execute on your microscopic daily goals. Telescope goals are 1,3,5+ years into the future and the microscope goals are what you will do in the next 24 hours to move towards your telescope goals. Remember, Inch by inch, goal setting is a cinch and yard by yard, it's hard."

I sat for a minute and thought. Coach Kenny was right. I had set this financial goal before I was married and had kids and it was still my #1 goal. I had not readjusted my telescope goals and for sure did not have any microscope goals for the next 24 hours that aligned with my telescope goals. I was putting finance over family and it was costing me more than any amount of money was worth. I couldn't even remember the last time I had kissed my wife, and the last thing my son Michael had said when I was walking out the door while on the phone was, "Daddy, why do you love your cell phone more than me?" My heart sank as my wife looked at me and said, "I was starting to wonder the same thing." It was like a one-two combination right to the gut.

"You make a lot of good points, Coach Kenny," I said. "I feel like you know me and we just met. Am I that easy to read?"

"Look, as humans we all wear our emotions somewhere," Coach Kenny said. "Some of us more than others. With you, I was able to see your stress in your breathing on the plane, your body language in the way you were walking in the airport and in how you are sitting right now. It's easy for me to see, but probably not as easy for others who are not MPM Coaches and as cued in on emotional intelligence as I am, and probably impossible for you to see in yourself. We are often the last to see in ourselves what everyone else sees. The only way to speed up that process is to have two things."

"What two things? A burger and a cream soda?" I chuckled.

"That helps," Coach Kenny laughed. "No, what you need are..."
 "Attention, Passengers on Northeast Airlines Flight 4824 from Detroit to Arizona," the

woman's voice said over the PA system as we both sat up straight and listened. "This flight has been canceled due to a mechanical issue. Please see an agent for rebooking on the next available flight."

My heart sank. I wasn't getting home anytime soon.

CHAPTER 4
THE TWO THINGS

"That sucks!" I yelled and slammed my fists on the table in another rage of frustration. Not only was I not going to get home for Thanksgiving, I was also going to miss Erin's birthday.

"What are you going to do about it?" Coach Kenny asked. "Are you going to sit here and continue to feel sorry for yourself or are you going to do something productive and see if you can get on that next plane or find another way home? Feeling sorry for yourself never did anyone any good and it won't serve well in this instance either. It's a worthless, useless emotion. Take a deep breath and enjoy your burger."

I took a deep breath, sighed, and again said, "That's a good point. You seem to be making a lot of those tonight."

"Look, you can focus on what is or you can focus on what if," Coach Kenny said. "If you focus on 'what if,' your mind plays tricks on you and you get lost because you get too far into the future or the past. If you get too far into the past you welcome depression and if you get too far into the future you bring on anxiety. Optimal performers stay in the present and focus on what is. They don't play the what if game. If you play the 'what is' game, you start to feel better because you can actually do something about what is and improve your situation."

"I called in earlier. The next seat they have on a plane back to Arizona isn't until Saturday," I said. "I am going to miss Thanksgiving with the kids and my wife's birthday. She is going to be pissed. She told me not to come on the last few days of this trip because of the holiday and how a few years ago I got stuck in Vermont and couldn't get home for Thanksgiving. I told her that's because it was Vermont and that the Detroit airport was much bigger and that delays never happen in Detroit. She is going to be pissed."

"And she is going to be right," Coach Kenny said. "If you had the option to go home earlier and didn't, your actions clearly show you value finance over family. You need the two things we were talking about before they made that announcement. These are the two things every great athlete and every great performer in any field has. Do you want to know what they are?"

"Yes, sir," I replied.

"You need a coach and an accountability partner. A coach to train you on *The 10 Pillars of Mental Performance Mastery* so that you can live a optimal life of excellence and fulfillment in all areas of your life, especially the big three of family, energy and service, and an accountability partner to help you stay on course and on target so that you don't drift so far to one side that you get lost," Coach Kenny said. "Right now, it seems like you have drifted too far to the financial side, which is a component of family, and because you are too far to the extreme, you are losing your family."

Coach Kenny was right. I served as a coach and accountability partner for people in my job, but didn't have either a coach or accountability partner for myself in my own life. I was not practicing what I teach and it was costing me.

I wondered if Coach Kenny would be my coach and accountability partner. Before asking him about that, I needed to call Erin and explain why I wasn't going to get home tonight. This was one phone call I didn't want to make.

As I stood up from the table and walked over to the side of the restaurant for some privacy, my palms started to sweat and my heart sank as I reached into my pocket for the phone.

CHAPTER 5
THE PHONE CALL

"Saturday! You can't get home till Saturday? I hate to tell you I told you so. But I told you so. I knew this was going to happen. I knew you would get stuck, Matthew. Thanks for missing Thanksgiving and my birthday… again!"

Those were exactly the words I was expecting to hear from Erin. She had a funny way of predicting what was going to happen. She was always talking about how everything happens twice and how Thoughts Become Things (TBT); that you attract to yourself what you think about most often; that energy flows where focus goes and when you focus on what you don't want, you get more of what you don't want. I was thinking a lot about how bad it would be if my flight got delayed and how terrible it would be if I didn't make it home. Ironically, that's exactly what happened.

"What am I supposed to tell Michael and Brina? Dad won't be home for Thanksgiving because he wants to work more than be with you?" Erin said as she fought back tears. "They already hardly know you because you are never home. They probably won't know any different anyway.

Can't you get in a car and drive home? Isn't there another flight? You always say that you can find a way or you can find an excuse but you can't do both.   Time to start living what you teach, Matthew."

As she hung up the phone I could feel the sadness, disappointment and frustration in her voice. I couldn't blame her. I didn't HAVE to come to Detroit; I chose to come.

Erin always says that when you say *yes* to one thing you say *no* to something else. She always challenged me to be aware of what I was saying *yes* to because I seemed to always say *no* to her and the kids. I knew I needed to start saying *no* to others so that I could say *yes* to them.

When I got back to the table, Coach Kenny was staring at his phone with a smile a mile wide.

I sat down, put my head into my hands and thought about how I was going to get home.

"I love you too, my sweet bear," Coach Kenny said.

I sat up and looked at Coach Kenny, wondering if he was speaking to me. Then he leaned over and kissed his phone.

"See you when I see you, but know you are always in my vision. Dominate The Day, Bear. I love you."

He then hung up the phone and reached for a French fry on his plate.

"Did you just kiss your phone?" I asked him, laughing.

"Sure did. Do it every night that I don't get to do it in person," Coach Kenny said. "Whenever I am on the road, I will send a morning selfie video wishing my wife Brittany, who I call Bear, a blessed day and then at night we FTK, which stands for FaceTime Kiss, and I tell her how much I love her. Those are key parts of our AM and PM routines and no matter how many days I am away, it's never too long when you get that FTK each night. Don't get me wrong; nothing is as good as the real thing."

FaceTime kiss, morning selfie videos. This guy was the Romeo of all Romeos. Why had I not thought of that? That seemed so simple, so easy to do, a great way for me to stay connected to Erin and the kids when I was on the road. There were days that I never spoke to any of them when on the road because they were still sleeping when I got started and back asleep by the time I was done with work for the day.

As I sat back in my chair, I looked across the table at a man who I felt could really help me.

I just needed to work up the courage to ask him for help as my coach and accountability partner.

CHAPTER 6
THE FIVE MAGIC WORDS

"Coach Kenny. Can you help me?" I asked with the look of a man who was beaten down by life and was feeling lost. "I know I just met you and all, but I feel like I could learn a lot from you. I feel like I have lost my direction, I feel like a total loser, and I need your help. Are you taking on any new clients?"

Coach Kenny sat up straight and took a sip of his cream soda. He leaned across the table and looked me straight in the eye with the focused stare that only an Olympic athlete could muster.

"Did you say you felt like a loser? Son, did you not hear what I said earlier about there being no such thing as a loser?" Coach Kenny asked. "In life, there are winners and learners. I can't help you if you are not willing to listen, and you can't help yourself if you are not willing to ask for help. As a coach, you can't help those who don't want to be helped. Ego is the enemy and most people let their pride and ego get in the way of progress. Asking for help is a sign of strength, a sign of humble confidence – the humility to know you don't have all the answers and the confidence to know that you are working to get better. And the most important thing anyone can do is have a rage for mastery, a passion for getting better, for learning and applying what you learn.

"Unfortunately, I'm not taking any new clients. However, if you allow me to buy you this dinner, I will share with you the philosophy and system that I learned while training to be an Olympian, which is the same system I use to train the people I work with to give themselves the best chance to be the best they can be and to give them the best chance for success," Coach Kenny said. "I call it *The 10 Pillars of Mental Performance Mastery.* I will work with you only if you are willing to listen and to apply. I don't have time for clients that don't listen, don't apply and don't make time for themselves because they use the excuse of being too busy."

"Coach Kenny, I will listen and I will apply. Thank you so very much," I said. "I have been thinking about what you said, about needing a coach and an accountability partner. I do that for other people; I just don't do it for myself. I will do what you coach me to do if you think it will help me get to where I want to be."

Coach Kenny then asked me one of the most difficult questions in the world.

"Let me ask you the five magic words, Matthew Simonds. What do you really want? We need to start there. What do you really want?"

As I took a deep breath, I realized that I had not been asking myself one of the most important questions that I ask my clients. I always started out my coaching sessions in the corporate world as I did earlier in my life when I was a personal trainer by asking my clients what they really wanted. I guess I never asked myself that same thing.

Now, more than ever, I needed to. I knew that if you didn't have clarity on what you really wanted you would NEVER end up with what you wanted and would always be chasing success vs. making progress towards becoming a successful person.

CHAPTER 7
WHAT DO YOU REALLY WANT?

"You must get clear on what you really want and you must get clear on how you define success for yourself. Otherwise you are playing on someone else's scoreboard vs. your scoreboard that you intentionally set," Coach Kenny stated. "Success is not what society wants you to think. It has nothing to do with the size of your house, the size of your bank account, the type of car you drive, how much your tailored suit cost or the number of places you have been for vacation. Success is purely to be measured by the individual and how that individual lives compared to the vision he or she holds of his or her best self. So again, Matthew Simonds, what do you really want, and how do you define success for yourself?"

I sat in silence. I had lost my vision for what I really wanted. I had no measurements for success. I was going through life on a mission to achieve my goal of financial security and I was risking what was most important to me – my family – in the process. I was also in the worst shape of my life at 240 lbs. and felt like I was lost in so many areas of life.

"I don't know what I really want, Coach Kenny," I replied dejectedly. "I thought I wanted to achieve a level of financial security, and I have let that goal consume me. I am losing my health and the ones I love in pursuit of that goal, and it's not worth it."

Coach Kenny then said something that hit me right between the eyes.

"Be careful of who you become in pursuit of what you want."

I thought about that for a minute. It was so profound. I was becoming a man I didn't want to be because of the pursuit of a goal. I ate, drank and gambled too much as a form of a stress release, and didn't exercise enough or spend enough time with my wife and kids. I was so busy trying to please and serve those outside of my house that I was sacrificing and neglecting those I cared about most who lived in my house. I was letting myself go vs. taking care of my family and working to be the best I could be in all areas.

"Again, Matthew Simonds. What do you really want?"

As I took a bite of my burger and a sip of my cream soda to buy some time, it hit me.

"What I really want is to be significant in the lives of my wife and kids, to be a great husband and father, to be significant in the lives of others and to do what I love to do, which is educate, empower and energize others to become their best."

Coach Kenny then handed me his cell phone and had me text what I really wanted to myself so that we both had it on our phones. It's crazy to think, but as I sent that text, it felt kind of like a weight was being lifted off my back.

"That's a great start, Matthew Simonds, and it's the start that stops most people. Clarity is key. You must know what you want, why you want it, who you currently are and who you need to become to get what you want." Coach Kenny said. "Now what we need to do is equip you with a toolbox of skills and drills and plan to help you grow into the type of person that can be significant in the lives of his wife and kids, be a great husband and father, and educate, empower and energize others to become their best.

"The start is to chart your destination. To fix your telescope goals on a target and know what you want. Now we must go to work on giving you the skills you need to be the best you can be to reverse engineer or simply work backwards starting with those telescope goals and working back to today in the microscope and then navigate the course to get you to your destination in that telescope. Basically, we need to game plan your process and the pathway to get your desired result.

"Always remember this: If you influence and impact others, you will make an income. You have focused on income first, and when you do that, you actually earn less because you lose focus on the influence and impact you have on others," Coach Kenny said. "Always keep influence and impact ahead of income and you will earn more. If you put income ahead of influence and impact, you won't get any of it and you will be miserable.

"We are going to focus on the best ways you can have influence and impact on others by starting with yourself. Remember, those you lead, both in your house and in your coaching, need a model to see and they need a motto to say," Coach Kenny stated. "My experience says that people need both a model and a motto, and the model always comes first. People need someone to emulate and follow, a role model. They also need to have short, powerful self-talk triggers we call mottos to come back to as a strategy to keep your focus on the process.

I am going to coach you on how to be the model for others to see in line with the vision for your future, and we're going to do that by taking you through my signature training system, *The 10 Pillars of Mental Performance Mastery.*"

CHAPTER 8
THE 10 PILLARS OF MENTAL PERFORMANCE MASTERY

I wanted to be a model for others to see, a leader for others to look to. I knew I was falling short in a lot of areas, especially in my own home. What Coach Kenny said made so much sense to me in such a short period of time. I was fired up to learn about *The 10 Pillars of Mental Performance Mastery*.

At the same time, I was torn. I felt like I should go get a rental car and start driving the 18+ hours or so it would take to get back home, or at least start the trip by checking into a hotel and getting some sleep, and then start the drive in the morning.

But I wanted more. Coach Kenny spoke in a way that resonated with me like my high school football coach John Allen.

Coach Allen was one of the first people to believe in me and to teach me about the importance of mental performance mastery. I had lost contact with Coach Allen, but never lost contact with his teachings. He was also MPM

Certified, I remembered seeing the certificate proudly displayed in his office and going through his summer Mental Performance Mastery Bootcamp, one pillar a day for 10 days, the two week period of football training camp that we all look forward to the most because it was where we learned life success through football.

"Matthew Simonds, *The 10 Pillars of Mental Performance Mastery* have been around forever. They are used and taught by the greatest achievers of all time. Not one person excels in all 10 of the pillars, yet I have seen a direct correlation with the success of individuals and groups and their commitment to growing in each of the 10 pillars," Coach Kenny said. "Growth is the key. Growth is the first step to mastery. If you keep growing, you will master. No pride, no ego, just progress and learning. Let's start with pillar #1, because I already know you need it."

CHAPTER 9
PILLAR #1
ELITE MINDSET

"Pillar #1 is understanding that you train an elite mindset just like you train your body or any other physical skill that you would use in sport or in business. The ideal way to train anything is through the process of (#1) a total immersion learning experience (TILE) followed by (#2) spaced repetition (SR), and that spaced repetition is called doing a little a lot, not a lot a little," Coach Kenny explained. "Whether it was training for the Olympics years ago or the work I currently do with top athletes and corporate executives, the total immersion, shock-your-system approach, followed by spaced repetitious follow-up and (#3) a growth plan that you share with an accountability partner and check in on daily or weekly, is ideal.

"An elite mindset is a mindset in which you are able to think the same way as the best of the best, which leads to a performance like the best of the best," Coach Kenny stated. "Let's look at some of the fundamental differences in thinking between average and elite performers.

"Performers with an average mindset use the phrase *have to*; those with an elite mindset use the words *get to* or *want to*.

"Performers with an average mindset focus on how they feel; those with an elite mindset focus on how they act and what they need to do, not how they feel about doing it. People with an elite mindset know that you don't wait for your feelings to change your actions; you focus on making your actions change your feelings.

"Performers with an average mindset make excuses; those with an elite mindset make it happen.

"Performers with an average mindset feel sorry for themselves; those with an elite mindset are so focused on others that they do not have time to feel sorry for themselves and know that feeling sorry for yourself is a worthless and useless emotion.

"Performers with an average mindset say it's impossible; those with an elite mindset say it's going to be very difficult.

"Performers with an average mindset see a failure as final, while those with an elite mindset see failure as positive feedback and every setback as a setup for a comeback.

"Performers with an average mindset wear their emotions on their sleeves; those with an elite mindset never show weakness and are always BIG with their body language so they can be the rock of confidence for others.

"Performers with an average mindset see confidence as a feeling; those with an elite mindset know that confidence is a choice and confidence is something you do, not just a feeling.

"Performers with an average mindset focus on what they can't control; those with an elite mindset focus on what they can control."

By this point I had taken my phone out of my pocket, flipped it on airplane mode and turned on the voice memos app to record the golden nuggets of wisdom Coach Kenny was sharing. I also started scribbling down on a napkin as fast as I could the most important ideas he was sharing.

"Coach Kenny, this is great stuff. How did you learn to think this way and build such a great mindset and perspective?" I asked.

"I didn't always think like this," Coach Kenny replied. "There are two primary mindsets: a fixed or average mindset and a growth or elite mindset. For a long time, I had a fixed mindset and thought that was the way I was and that was it. That my success and achievement was because of my talent. When I got around some of the other talented athletes training for the Olympics, I changed. I was physically gifted, but mentally I was behind. Being around the other athletes and some really good coaches opened up my eyes to a new way of thinking, and a growth mindset emerged. I started to see success as a result of training, attitude, hard work and preparation, not just inborn talent.

"Now I try to read a book a month and put into action what I learn. I just can't get enough. I wish I had taken this approach to learning when I was your age. I know I don't have a lot of time left to live, but I am going to learn like I will live forever. I am going to live a lot in the time I do have left and I am going to give away as much as I can. I can't take anything up here with me to the grave so I might as well give it all away," Coach Kenny said as he pointed to his head.

I thought about how elite of a mindset he must have and how much more to this new way of thinking there must be. I related more to examples of the performers with an average mindset than I did to those with an elite mindset and I wanted to change. I wanted to grow my elite mindset.

Coach Kenny then excused himself to take a phone call.

I overheard his conversation as he picked up the volume of his voice.

"Six months – well, that's better than a year, brother. Stay positive and remember that your attitude determines your altitude and that the more positive you are, the faster the body heals. Be strong. Attack your rehab and never feel sorry for yourself. Knees heal. Compared to what it could have been, you are lucky. Remember that keeping a *compared to what* mindset will help keep you from feeling sorry for yourself. Now dominate rehab, one day at a time."

As he hung up, he took a deep breath and said to me, "Injuries suck. Especially the freak ones."

"If you don't mind me asking, what happened?" I wanted to know.

"One of my clients is a world champion mixed martial artist and had a big title fight coming up next month. He was jumping on a trampoline with his kids when the tramp springs broke and he fell to the ground. Luckily, he was the only one on that part of the tramp and his kids are fine, but he tore his ACL and is now out for at least 6 months," Coach Kenny said. "I told him to stay strong, to stay positive – that negativity only slows down recovery and that if he started to feel sorry for himself to simply think of a *compared to what* scenario to help get his mind right.

"Compared to what could have happened if it was his kids that fell through the tramp and not him," Coach Kenny continued. "It could have been a whole lot worse. He will be fine. I feel for him, yet at the same time everyone else is going to feel sorry for him, and he can't let himself feel sorry for himself. Feeling sorry for yourself is a worthless emotion. He needs to remember that his attitude determines his altitude and that the attitude he takes is always a decision he makes. Your attitude is a decision, maybe the most important one you will ever make."

As I grabbed for another napkin to write down *the attitude you take is a decision you make*, I was reminded of something that Coach Allen used to teach us in his summer football mental performance mastery boot camp that I understood more the older I got.

He used to tell us that the more energy we gave the more energy we would get. That energy was a life cycle and if your energy was negative, you would get more negative energy and negative performance, and if your energy was positive, you would get more positive energy and positive performance. He said life was an energy management game, that energy attracts and energy is contagious. He would then ask if our energy was worth catching or avoiding.

Coach Kenny sure fit this mold and at 70 years old, I was starting to think he might be the most energetic person I had ever met.

"How do you stay so positive?" I asked him.

"You know, I wasn't always the most positive guy, especially when I was younger," Coach Kenny said. "I am a learned optimist. I have learned the power of positive thinking and I have learned to have an attitude of gratitude.

"One of my clients, a professional baseball player, sent me a video of a guy he had worked with in mental performance mastery in baseball when he was playing in college at TCU. The video was of this coach, talking about The GHP Principle and was a part of a video series called *The Monday Message*. I am sure you can find it on YouTube by doing a search for *The Monday Message*, GHP Principle," Coach Kenny said.

"The GHP Principle is that if you express more gratitude, you will experience more happiness and that will lead to a better performance. The principle states that as gratitude goes up, so does your happiness and so does your performance," Coach Kenny explained. "I started an *Attitude of Gratitude* journal on my phone and every day I simply write down one thing I'm grateful for. This has been like lifting weights for my elite mindset, positive energy and happiness. Matthew Simonds, you have got to start keeping an *Attitude of Gratitude* journal."

I was thinking the same thing after hearing Coach Kenny speak with such enthusiasm about his *Attitude of Gratitude* journal.

"You know, being positive, grateful and having an elite mindset is the start. Being juiceful means you are useful to the world and if you are juiceless, well, you are useless. But bringing the juice is just not enough; it's a lot, but not all," Coach Kenny said. "Having an elite mindset is like having a $100,000 sports car in your garage. When you look at it, it's amazing. It sounds impressive when you rev the engine. The only problem is that if you don't put tires on that car, it's not going to take you anywhere.

"The tires are your skill set in all 10 pillars. The tires are the strategies that you implement. The car is your motivational speaker who gets you pumped, but you don't have any performance change because you don't know what to do. The mental performance mastery (MPM) certified coach is the strategist who actually tells you how to do what the motivational speaker tells you that you must do.

That's the different between a speaker and a mental performance mastery coach. The motivational speaker will say you must have an elite mindset, be a leader, have the right culture etc. It's the mental performance mastery coach who actually shows you HOW do build these skills.

To play off the car analogy, the skills of the 10 pillars of mental performance mastery make up the car, the drills to go to work on developing the 10 pillars are the tires that allow you to drive. The engine is your leadership skills and your MVP process and culture is the GPS that assures you arrive at your destination. Without your GPS and MVP process you will just drive in circles, even if you have all of the other skills from the 10 pillars of mental performance mastery on lock down," Coach Kenny said.

I was a little confused. What did he mean, *your personal and organizational MVP process?*

CHAPTER 10
PILLAR #9
LEADERSHIP

"The MVP is your Mission, Vision and Principles," Coach Kenny explained. "Great leaders know their personal MVP process and great organizations have an organizational MVP process that serves as the backbone of their culture, the safety net for when things get hard – and the only guarantee is that things will get hard. Once you have developed an elite mindset, then you want to work on growing your leadership skills. Once you have the leadership skills, you then want to go to work on creating the right culture in your organization, which might be your team, your company or your family, or finding the organization with the right culture if you are a free agent looking for employment.

You will learn why I put Leadership as Pillar #9 and not Pillar #2 later. The key with all of the Pillars is understanding that there is tremendous overlap, that all of these pillars build off each other and create a lifestyle of excellence and optimal living. Think of them as one large Venn Diagram.

"Leadership starts with having your own personal MVP process and knowing who you are and what you want. Who you are is your mission and core principles, and what you want is your vision. You want to have a telescope vision for your life and a microscope vision for the day, the week, the month and the quarter. If you don't have a mission, vision and core principles to guide your life, you have no foundation to lead from. You won't show up consistently because you don't have clarity on who you are, and you won't be able to use the skills you develop through mental performance mastery as they are intended to be used because you won't have the foundation and the vision for who you are, what you want and why you are here."

"Leadership is a never-ending field. Go to Amazon and there are thousands of books on leadership. Let me simplify this for you, Matthew Simonds," Coach Kenny said.

"Thank you. I have heard more speakers and been given more books on leadership than I can remember, and the more I hear or read the more confused I get," I responded.

"Well, let's simplify leadership," Coach Kenny said. "One of the greatest football coaches of all time, Urban Meyer, wrote in his great book *Above the Line* about simplifying leadership. I totally agree with what Urban has written and you can't deny his success. He says leadership is about your ability to do two fundamental things: (1) Build trust and (2) get results.

"Trust is a by-product of your ability to (#1) build connection with the people you lead, (#2) have the competence to help them close the gap from where they are to where they want to be and (#3) to show up with character consistently and ethically the same way so they know what they are getting with their leader. This is why the personal MVP process is so important. You have to know who you are if you are going to connect, be consistent and be competent. You have to know who you are to lead based off of principle (a set of values and standards) vs. preference (a set of feelings in the moment).

"If you want to get results, you have to help those you lead gain (#1) clarity so they know specifically what to do and what's expected of them. You also have to provide (#2) accountability and (#3) support. As a Mental Performance Mastery coach, I have had clients stay with me for over 10 years. They are not paying me for new information; they are paying me for accountability and support and to help them maintain clarity so they can get results.

It's lonely at the top and as leaders to some of the best coaches and athletes who are at the top, they know they need the accountability and support from a neutral party who has their best interest in mind and will not tell them what they want to hear but will tell them what they *need* to hear. I couldn't serve in a leadership position for these people if I didn't have a personal MVP process to drive my own behavior.

"Your Mission, Vision and Principles – your MVP process – make up your leadership philosophy for you individually, and when you do it organizationally, it sets the foundation for the culture. Leadership determines culture, culture drives your decisions and behaviors, and your behaviors and decisions determine your results. Meyer calls this *The Performance Pathway.* You must have an MVP process for yourself as a leader, for your organizational culture, for your family and your business. If you don't, you will crumble.

"With no MVP process, you will get distracted by the noise, the glitz and the glamour as you climb the ladder of success. You will look at Twitter, Instagram, Facebook and other media outlets and compare yourself to what others are doing and second-guess and question yourself, which will be your demise.

Consistency WINS. I have seen all different types of people and teams win; those that do are consistent and they implement the 10 pillars of mental performance mastery whether they are intentional about doing it or not, they do it.

With no MVP process, you will stall out when you get put into a leadership position where you have people counting on you, just like you are right now, Matthew Simonds."

Coach Kenny was right. I had no mission, no vision and no core principles. I was on the treadmill of life. Just running through the motions, running away or towards something – which one I wasn't sure. I just knew I was running and it was not in the direction I wanted to go; I just didn't know how to turn it around. I was not building trust with those I cared about and the results I was getting were not the results I truly wanted.

"You know, Matthew Simonds, one of my running coaches used to say to me: *Kenny, running is an individual sport. Life is a team sport. You must invest in developing your leadership and relationships.* He would say that even though you compete in the decathlon as an individual, there are no individual sports, that there are no individual athletes and no self-made men or women. We all need a team and we must invest into our leadership and relationship skills, or, like muscles unattended to, they will become weak.

"That same coach had us measure the number of high fives we gave to our teammates at the track. At the time, I was young and thought this was stupid. Now, I give out high fives as much as I can because I have seen how much physical contact can enhance a relationship and build connection between two people and increase energy. High fives are also free."

Just as he said that, Coach Kenny reached across the table and gave me a high five. Then he spun around and said to our waitress, "Hey, Lynn, you are standing in a high five zone," and he gave her one as well. I wondered, "How did he know her name?"

When he sat back down and laughed, the smile on his face was a mile wide.

"The beautiful bear [Coach Kenny's wife] and I started a high five zone in our house when our kids were little, and every time we walked by them in that space we would high five."

"Kind of like mistletoe during the holidays?" I asked.

"Just like mistletoe, only for leadership and relationships. The Bear and I actually have a piece of mistletoe hanging up in our bedroom year-round. It is a constant reminder for us of the importance of physical contact. We also still use the high five zone in our house, even now when it's just the two of us. When the grandkids come over, they will stand in the high five zone for hours, counting how many they can get. It's a lot of fun."

As I thought more about it, Coach Allen used to encourage us to make contact with our teammates when coming on and off the field. It finally made sense why. After hearing Coach Kenny talk, it all started to make sense. It was about connection, building relationships and through that, increasing trust.

"There was a study done at a school in California. They kept track of the number of times teammates in the NBA made physical contact with each other during a game," Coach Kenny said. "What they found was that the more a team touched, the more they won. I have shared that article with all of the coaches and athletes I work with. The ones that embrace contact with each other and make it a part of their routine win more games. It's such a simple concept and so powerful. Usually it's the simple things that win, especially today when as a society we are very sensitive to human touch and spend almost all of our waking hours touching a screen with our fingers and never coming in contact with another human physically. Check out the research on the 20 second hug when you can. It's powerful."

The more I thought about it, the more sense it made to me. Leadership was about relationships, and to be consistent in relationships you needed to know who you were and have an MVP process.

CHAPTER 11
PILLAR #10
THE RIGHT CULTURE

Then it dawned on me. I went back to a time when I was getting results and I was a part of a great culture with great leadership.

"You know, Coach Kenny," I said, "when I played high school football, Coach Allen was the best leader I had ever been around at that point in my life and he also created a tremendous culture. He actually set up an MVP process for us as a program and a team. I never thought about doing that for myself or with my family."

"Do you remember what your MVP process was on your high school football team?" Coach Kenny asked. "Do you know if Coach Allen had a personal MVP process that he used to help lead or just an organizational one?"

I wasn't sure if he had a personal MVP process, but I'd assume he must have. Amazingly, I could clearly remember the team's MVP process. It was 22 years ago and I can recall it as clear as day. Coach Allen used to model it, teach it and demand that we live it every day.

"I can. He used to say that our mission was to be men who lived principle- and not preference-based lives on and off the field. Our vision was to win the day, win the league, win the district and win the state championships every year. Our core principles were the acronym DELT, to have disciplined daily habits and actions, to bring a positive energy and pursue personal and team excellence, to love each other and the process and to be trustworthy people who did what they said they would do and do what was right."

As I spoke about the mission, vision and principles Coach Allen shared with us during my high school football experience, I started getting emotional and the hair started sticking up on my body. I had been a part of a lot of teams in my life, both in athletics and in business, but none were as close as my high school football team and nobody had led us through building trust and getting results better than Coach Allen. Some of my teammates were the best men in my wedding, the godfathers of my children, in attendance at my mother's funeral, and some of my closest friends still, 22 years later – especially my center, Ross Ackley. We trade books on an annual basis and I actually had a book in my book called *Make Your Bed* that he had sent me.

"Coach Allen used to tell us that the difference between a boy and a man was that a boy made decisions out of preference and a man made decisions out of principle," I said. "He challenged us every day to be men of principle and to live out the core principles (DELT) of our program and play the hand we were DELT. I think as I get older, I realize more and more that he was teaching us not only how to win football games, but also how to win in life."

"Matthew Simonds, there is a tremendous crossover from what makes athletes and teams successful on the field to what makes people successful in life. The skills I learned in being an Olympic athlete have given me everything I have achieved outside of athletics," Coach Kenny stated. "Have you ever thought about setting a mission, vision and principles for yourself and your family so that you can better lead yourself and your family?"

I was embarrassed. I had never even thought of doing this. I knew that 50%+ of marriages ended in divorce, and I bet almost all of the 50%+ did not have a mission, vision and principles that served as the foundation of their marriage.

"Your mission has no finish line. This is the bigger-picture purpose for your life; think about this as your eulogy or what you want your teammates to say about you when you retire or the season is over."

"Your vision is what you want to accomplish based on long-term results. Think about your vision as more of your résumé or your goals; long-term goals are your telescope goals and short-term goals are the microscope goals. We need both."

"Your core principles are like core values or character traits and serve as the map that you follow on a daily basis to help achieve your mission and your vision," Coach Kenny stated. "Matthew Simonds, if I could give you one gift, it would be that you get clarity on your personal MVP process and the MVP process for your family."

I was finally starting to see how the MVP process came together and I needed one... *yesterday*. I was just lacking the motivation and commitment I needed to get going.

CHAPTER 12
PILLAR #2
MOTIVATION AND COMMITMENT

"Let's move on from pillar #9 leadership and pillar #10 culture and talk about what you need after having an elite mindset, it's pillar #2 motivation and commitment.

Why do you think there are Olympic records?" Coach Kenny asked.

"So that we can experience the excitement of the chase and the exhilaration that comes from breaking a record?" I responded.

"It's much easier than that," Coach Kenny replied. "We keep records because they provide motivation and enhance commitment. Measurement is motivation.

"In athletics, we keep all sorts of statistics to help measure how one performer matches up with another. In business, we focus on our essential metrics, and in education we make data-driven decisions," Coach Kenny said. "To accurately measure your progress and growth, you must know your numbers, and evaluating your numbers must become a routine part of your system."

The only number I ever measured was my bank account – how close I was to reaching my goal of financial security. I really needed to start measuring things like how much I was home, how many times I played with the kids, had dinner with my wife, and more personal and relationship metrics vs. just business.

"You have to be careful, though, with your numbers, because you can do anything but you can't do everything," Coach Kenny said. "Starting with a few measurements done daily is better than trying to measure too many things at once. Doing a little a lot, not a lot a little, is the key to motivation and commitment. You also have to realize that not everything that matters can be measured, and not everything that can be measured matters. You must find the right numbers to measure."

"Do you have numbers that you measure on a routine basis as a part of your motivation and commitment system?" I asked.

"I sure do." Kenny beamed. "I measure how much sleep I get; if I sent The Bear a nice message; what time I woke up; if The Bear and I FTK'd at night when I am on the road; if I exercised that day; what I ate that day in terms of the macro nutrients fat, carb and protein grams; if I did a form of meditation; how many phone calls to my friends I made; whether I called The Success Hotline (973-743-4690); if I read *The Daily Dominator;* and how I felt my overall presence was with people that day."

Coach Kenny had a presence and a laser-like focus that I had never experienced. When he was with you, it felt like you were the only person in the room. He had the perfect blend of intensity that you would get from an Olympic athlete and the sincerity and love you would get from your grandfather. Unlike many of the people I worked with who seemed to care more about looking at their phones than they did the people they were with; Coach Kenny had not touched his phone since I met him other than when he was FTK-ing his wife. His presence was impressive.

"I simply keep a checklist with me by my bed and fill it out each morning when I wake up. I then go over it with my accountability partner, best friend, teammate and wife – the lovely and beautiful Brittany "The Bear"," Coach Kenny said as his face lit up with love.

"She is my rock, my everything. We have been together ever since we trained together for the Olympics. She has taught me more about mindset, leadership, culture, motivation, and commitment than anyone I know. She works back home in Paradise Valley as a yoga instructor, and she really takes measurements to another level. She measures how many students come in each day, week, month, quarter and year. She measures how many times she says *thank you*, how many times she makes a home-cooked meal. She loves her numbers and she is my #1. She also has her students measure their progress in their home practice and report back to her at the start of each of her sessions, and I think this is the secret to her success. A student of hers once is a student for life. We share that mentality; it's part of what drives our motivation and commitment to serve others and keep working to be the best version of ourselves."

As I sat there listening to him talk about his wife, I knew I needed to start measuring some sort of relationship deposit into my family. I needed to have a plan to rekindle the relationships I had neglected with Erin, Brina and Michael. I loved them and our twin French bulldogs Yotie and Cypress. We had named them after where Erin and I went on our first date, an Arizona Coyotes hockey game, and where I had proposed to her, at the Lone Cypress in Pebble Beach, California. I was determined to start measuring something – I just didn't know where to start.

"Coach Kenny, I know you said it was the start that stops most people. I want to get started with measuring something that will improve my relationships at home. I'm just at a bit of a loss; do you have any suggestions?"

"Well, I sure do," Kenny replied with a smile. "But, before we start measuring, let's set the target for your measurements by getting clarity on what you want, why you want it, your telescope goals for life and microscope goals or the rest of this quarter and let's have you then make a vision board, a collage of everything that you want to that you can see it on a daily basis. There is power in pictures. Once we have those drills done your motivation and commitment will be at an all-time high and then we can start by measuring your presence, your focus and awareness because if you are present, focused and aware, you will increase your chances of sustaining that motivation and commitment at their all-time high."

CHAPTER 13
PILLAR #3
FOCUS AND AWARENESS

"Your focus determines your future and your presence is the greatest gift you can give anything or anyone," Coach Kenny said. "Yesterday is history. Tomorrow, that's a mystery. Today is a gift – that's why we call it the present. Matthew Simonds, you must learn to be more present, to be where your feet are, so that you can experience each moment at the highest level. To get present and stay present requires a high level of focus and awareness skill development."

Erin had always given me a hard time about hearing what she was saying but not listening to her, or for being there but not being present. I was starting to understand what she meant.

"Focus and awareness are the keys that unlock all doors. You can do anything with the right focus," Coach Kenny continued. "My grandson Reno is a football player for the Wente High School football team, which I think is one of the best, if not the best, high school football programs in the nation. Just the other day he was complaining about how bad the officials were in the last game and about how he felt like he was not getting a fair shot at the position he wanted to play, was not going to get a varsity letter or get to play at BJCC University of Arkansas for Coach Tony Love, his dream school, etc., etc. I wasn't having any of it.

"I told him, 'Reno, you need to make a choice. You are either going to get bitter, or you are going to get better. That's up to you to decide. Your focus determines your future and right now your focus is NOT fixed on what you want for your future so you WON'T get it, unless you get your mind right.'"

Coach Kenny fired up from his seat and stepped to the side of the table.

"I told him that his problem was that he had one foot in the past, one foot in the future, and that he was dumping all over this present moment," Coach Kenny said as he got down into a squat like a person going to the bathroom in the woods. "'You are beating yourself, son. You don't have to win a game or win a job; you just have to win a play today, that's all. Go do that!' He got the point."

I started laughing, harder than I had laughed in a long time as Coach Kenny, still squatting, said again, "He was dumping all over the greatest gift there is, the gift of this present moment. Dump, dump, dump, just going to the bathroom all over the greatest gift he could give."

Coach Kenny then stood up and reached into his backpack and took out a magnifying glass, something I hadn't seen in years.

"To further make my point about the importance of focus and awareness," Coach Kenny said, "I took him out to the backyard where, in Paradise Valley, Arizona, it was still a cool 105 degrees in fall. I took a magnifying glass and handed it to him. I said, 'Son, take the glass and move it around so that the sun goes through the glass and makes a little rainbow-colored circle on the ground. Then move that circle around and around on the grass and watch what happens.'

"Obviously, nothing happened," Coach Kenny said. "Then I had him get that rainbow-colored dot to stay on one piece of grass for a good minute. You know what happened? The grass started to burn. Smoke rose up and the grass caught on fire.

"That's exactly how your focus works. That's the gift of the present. For Reno, that was playing football one play at a time and living in the moment. Enjoying where he was at and what he was doing, not focusing so much on where he wanted to go and what he wanted to become that he missed this precious, present moment which is all he could control and influence.

"For you Matthew Simonds, that is showing up with a presence and a focus that you have never brought before. It's a 100% commitment to the moment, to the people you are with, to your family, to your customers, to totally being where your feet are. There is no greater gift you can give yourself or others than your presence."

I couldn't agree more. In the rare chance I got to go see Michael play football, I spent more time on my phone setting up my fantasy football team than I did watching him play. I spent more time in my car listening to sports talk radio about the Professional Football League (PFL) than I did listening to audio books or podcasts that would help me learn to become more. I was learning from Coach Kenny that if I wanted more I must become more, and that you didn't have to be sick to get better.

As Coach Kenny sat back down in his chair, he took a sip of his cream soda and asked, "You know why it's so hard to be present?"

"Because of this?" I answered pointing to my cell phone. "Because we are on call 24/7?"

"No. A cell phone is a tool that can actually help you to be more present if you use it right. It puts the world at your fingertips. That's helpful," Coach Kenny said. "The reason why it's so hard to be present is because of two things: (#1) We lack awareness of what it's like to be quiet minded and fully present and (#2) we focus on the wrong things, and we attract more of what we focus on. If you let yourself get distracted by your cell phone because you are like a dog on a digital leash or a gold fish that see's the castle in his fish bowl for the first time 1,000 times, that's because you lack self-control and discipline; don't blame that on the phone.

"Let's talk about awareness or what I call ATW – Awareness To Win. Awareness is knowing what's happening around you, to you and inside of you at all times. It's being able to respond to your response. It's being able to check in on your mental and emotional states and then having the ability to adjust them accordingly to keep yourself in the best state for a peak performance in that moment."

I was a little lost. I wasn't totally following what he was saying. I didn't want to show Coach Kenny that I couldn't totally understand what he was talking about because I didn't want him to think I wasn't with him. Then I remembered what Burt Watson, a friend and a legend in the mixed martial arts world, said once: *The only dumb question is the one you don't ask.*

"Coach Kenny, I am not sure I totally understand awareness to win," I said. "Can you explain it more? I want to know what it is so that I can live all of *The 10 Pillars of Mental Performance Mastery*."

"Matthew Simonds, think about awareness as a signal light when you are driving a car. When you get to the signal light, if it's green, it tells you to go. If it's red, it tells you to stop. If it's yellow, it tells you to slow down or speed up," Coach Kenny said with a chuckle. "Awareness is just like driving that car. In life, when you are in a positive state, feel good, are getting results and like the way things are rolling for you, we call that a green-light state.

"When you are in a negative state and things are moving really fast or slow for you, you don't feel good, and you are not getting the results you want, we call that a red-light state. Most of the time in life we operate in a yellow light state. We are in neutral and we either move ourselves towards a positive, green light state or a negative, red light state based on what we choose to focus on, how we choose to speak to ourselves and how we choose to carry ourselves physically.

"Matthew Simonds, please stand up, please stand up. Would the real Matthew Simonds please stand up, please stand up?" Coach Kenny said this in rhythm to the song "Slim Shady" by Eminem.

"You listen to Eminem?" I asked while laughing.

"Look, when you work the athletes and clients like I do, you have to read what they read, watch what they watch and listen to what they listen to or you'll miss on some connection points and become extinct," Coach Kenny said. "Eminem gets me fired up; I will listen to his stuff when I play *Fortnite* and when I run – that is, when I am not listening to an audio book, which is what I do 90% of the time. Audio books as I run – yes sir, that's another key part of building my elite mindset, increasing my motivation and commitment and sharpening my focus and awareness."

I laughed standing there. Here I was, out of shape, 40 years old and finding every excuse in the world to not run or do yoga, which Erin and the kids did together almost every day, and this 70-year-old savage was running every day, listening to audio books and Eminem, keeping a journal, playing *Fortnite* and living life at the highest level.

"Matthew Simonds. Now that you are standing, I want you to stand big and tall and pull your shoulders back. Now close your eyes and think of a time in your life when you were at your best," Coach Kenny said with a strong and positive tone.

I thought of the last vacation Erin and I had taken. We were on a cruise with friends to the Bahamas. This was before the kids were born. We were out on the dance floor having a great time moving together to a song by DJ Gulian called "Back That Azz Up." It was one of the most fun times of my life and probably the last time I had danced full out without a care in the world of what other people were thinking or saying. As I put myself back on that boat and on that dance floor, I could feel myself getting bigger, smiling wider and getting into a green light state.

"That's it," Coach Kenny said. "That's the green-light state. I can see it in you. Can you feel it?"

I nodded my head and opened my eyes.

"Good. Now I want you to close your eyes again and think of a time when you were at your worst, a time when you were in a red-light state," Coach Kenny said with a depressed tone of voice.

This was much easier for me. It had been a long time ago that I was in a true green light state. All I had to do to bring back a red-light state was remembering how my phone call with Erin, just an hour or so earlier, made me feel after she told me how disappointed she and the kids were that it looked like I was not going to be home for Thanksgiving or her birthday. I immediately felt my shoulders slump and my head go down from where it was when I was in the green light state. I felt much smaller.

"Do you feel that difference?" Coach Kenny asked.

"Yes, I feel smaller and heavier than I did in the green-light state," I said. "I feel like this is how I live most of the time."

"Not any more, you don't," Coach Kenny responded as he stood up from the table, put his two hands on my shoulders and looked me straight in the eye.

"You are in charge of your states at all times. You can get back to this green-light state anytime you want. Your states never leave you. They are always inside of you. You have the responsibility to learn how to get yourself into a green-light state all the time. Go green for yourself, for Erin, for Brina, for Michael, for the people you serve on your mission as a consultant. People are counting on you to be in green lights, Matthew Simonds. Your family needs you to be at your best. The people you serve need you to be at your best. The world needs you to be at your best, Matthew Simonds! You can't be normal; you must be elite. This world is littered with normal and average; don't allow yourself to get pulled into their world. Do *YOU!*" When you are average you are the best of the worst and the worst of the best, it's a terrible place to live.

I don't know why, but tears started pouring out of my eyes and I was overcome with emotion as I stood there in the Detroit airport Protector Brewery and Burger restaurant with Coach Kenny's hands on my shoulders. I felt a flood of emotion that I had not felt in years. I had learned to bury my feelings, to just put my head down and keep grinding. It was like all those years of keeping those emotions inside were coming out of me.

"I just don't know how to get out of the red-light state. I feel like such a loser," I said fighting through the tears and the emotion.

"Matthew Simonds, my friend, it's our focus that determines our future. Unfortunately, most people make the critical mistake that prevents them from being able to live in the present moment, and that critical mistake is they focus on the outcome they want instead of the process. The process is the pathway to get the outcomes they want, and you are making this same mistake. You are dumping on the present, my friend. Look, results are real, we get evaluated by results, however, it's the process that determines the results. Let's jump ahead to Pillar #5 and talk about process over outcome."

Coach Kenny then made me get into a squat with him and make a dumping sound. My tears of frustration and disappointment with myself turned into laughter as we both embraced and sat back down at the table. I can only imagine what the other people in the Protector Brewery and Burger must have been thinking… only this time I didn't care what they were thinking. In the past, I would have. Maybe this was the first sign that I was developing an elite mindset.

CHAPTER 14
PILLAR #5
PROCESS OVER OUTCOME

"Matthew Simonds, you may be wondering why we are jumping around in the pillars vs. going through them sequentially. Let me tell you why. Because the pillars are universal and can be thought in any order depending on what you assess that your clients, athletes or teams need. I put then in an order of 1-10 so that we could speak about them in a framework and so that the people I certify as MPM coaches would know a logical progression to follow, but you can also follow the flow that presents itself in your client meetings as we are doing here." Coach Kenny said.

"I am glad you like football, Matthew Simonds. It's my favorite sport to watch," Coach Kenny said. "One of my clients, Tony Love is a big-time college football coach and his whole program is based on process over outcome. His whole program is based on putting the process over the result."

Process over the result? I didn't quite understand. In college football, just as in my line of work as a business consultant, you were measured on one thing: results – wins and losses in football and bottom-line profits in business.

"What do you mean, Coach Kenny?" I asked. "Isn't it all about the win, about getting the outcome you want?"

Coach Kenny responded, "In the circles I run in, WIN stands for 'What's Important Now', and what's always important now is focusing on what you can control in that moment, being present, sticking to your process and being productive. Learn to let go of what you can't control and focus on what you can in that moment – that's the process. That's the formula for success. That's also the mistake that most people make in performance – they focus on what they can't control more often than what they can control and they beat themselves.

"Tony Love has three laws that we came up with together, that he uses with his team on a daily basis to reinforce the process, and I want to share these with you. So, please grab another napkin and write down these three laws because you need to know them."

I reached for another napkin and was glad that I had been recording this entire conversation. I was going to listen to this again to make sure I was picking up all of what Coach Kenny was putting down. I was also going to buy a notebook and transfer all my napkins to paper or do it in a Google Doc so I could always have it on my phone with me. If I were prepared, I would have had a notebook with me, or had Google Docs installed on my phone or a charged laptop that I could start typing notes on. Another sign I needed to raise my commitment in all areas of life.

"Are you ready?" Coach Kenny asked.

"Ready to roll," I answered.

"OK, here are three laws of the process from one of the best coaches in the world:

1. You must be in control of yourself before you can control your performance.
2. You have very little control of what goes on around you, but total control of how you choose to respond to it.
3. Your goal must be in your control.

"Matthew Simonds, in my 50+ years as a Mental Performance Mastery Coach and in my work with coaches and athletes of all ages, I can tell you this: The #1 pitfall that performers fall into is focusing on what they can't control more than what they can," Coach Kenny stated. "When you, or anyone for that matter, is focusing on what you can't control, you are beating yourself; you are playing with one hand tied behind your back.

"Let's get super clear here. I want you to make a list on your napkin of all the things you can't control, that if you keep focusing on will make you beat yourself. Then I want you to list what you can control on a separate napkin. While you do that, I am going to the bathroom."

Coach Kenny excused himself from the table and I started writing.

As I started to write my list of things I couldn't control, I was blown away by how long it was.

As I wrote my list of what I could control, I was shocked at how short it was.

I was really only in control of myself, my attitude and actions, my preparation and performance, my posture or body language, effort, energy and emotions.

"Matthew Simonds, here's what I want you to do," I heard Coach Kenny say over my shoulder as he returned from the bathroom. "Take that list of what you can't control, take it to the bathroom with you and flush it down the toilet. That's exactly what you need to do with what you can't control. You need to flush it!"

I liked where he was going. I needed to go to the bathroom, and I wanted to let go of all the stuff I couldn't control and focus on what I could. There was just one problem. I had put Erin, Brina, Michael, Yotie, and Cypress on the list of non-controllables and was not about to flush them down the toilet.

"Coach Kenny, where do you put your family? You can't really control them, can you? But I don't want to flush them down the toilet either."

"They are in your area of influence," he said. "There are aspects of life that you can control, areas that you can't control and areas that you can influence. Right now, we want to get you focused on what you can control and to let go of what you can't control and those things that you can only influence, for now, put them on the list of what you can't control. We need to get you 100% back to a focus and awareness of the process and of what you can control.

"You are right in that you can't control what your wife, kids and dogs do – but you can control how much of yourself that you invest into them, and you can control your response to what they do and what they say. If you maximize what you can control, you should be able to have maximum impact and influence with them. Tony Love gives his players a rubber wrist band like this as a constant reminder."

Coach Kenny rolled up his sleeve and showed me a white silicone band around his wrist that had E+R=O written on it in black.

"I first saw E+R+O in Jack Canfield's book *The Success Principles.* Urban Meyer also talks about E+R=O in *Above the Line* and it's a staple that Dr. Rob Gilbert teaches on *Success Hotline*. The bracelet is a reminder for Event + Response = Outcome. We are not in control of the events that happen day to day and we don't control the outcome, but we always control the response we take in any situation, and that will influence the outcome," Coach Kenny explained. "We must focus on our response. Viktor Frankl wrote about choosing your response to adversity in *Man's Search for Meaning,* Marcus Luttrell wrote about this in *The Lone Survivor,* and Louis Zamperini demonstrated this through his story *Unbroken.*

"Focusing on what you can control, on your response and on the process gives you the best chance for success and for getting the outcome you want," Coach Kenny stated. "The crazy thing is, you get less outcome when you focus on outcome. You get more outcome when you focus on process. When you focus on the outcome you sabotage your ability to perform. When you let go of the need to have something, you dramatically increase your chances of getting it."

I had all of those books he mentioned but had never read them. I typically read for entertainment, not for education. I should have read them as a man on a mission to find something of value that I could apply to my life. Even if I had read them, I would have missed those critical points.

Controlling what you can control. Focusing not on the events or the outcome, but on your response to those events. I loved it, and I wanted to live it. As I got up from the table to go to the restroom to flush the napkin where I had written down all of the things I could not control, I started to think about what I was going to do next.

I was still in Detroit. It was Wednesday and I still had no plan for how I was getting home.

It looked like my next flight wasn't until Saturday. I was loving my time with Coach Kenny, but I wanted to get home now more than ever. I thought hard about getting a rental car and driving the 18+ hours back to Paradise Valley, Arizona. If I had to sleep in the car, I could; it wouldn't be the first time. I was determined to get home and make this right. I knew I could either find a way or find an excuse. But first, I was going to find out what the rest of *The 10 Pillars of Mental Performance Mastery* were all about. I had a feeling the last four were going to be as life changing for me as the first six. I also wanted to learn how to get certified as a MPM Coach in Coach Kenny's system.

CHAPTER 15
PILLAR #4
SELF-CONTROL AND DISCIPLINE

When I got back to the table and sat down, Coach Kenny started right into me.

"You know, Matthew Simonds, what you don't have is exactly what the best coaches and athletes I work with have more than anyone else," Coach Kenny said. "It's trainable. It's also, with focus and awareness, one of the most difficult of all the 10 pillars to develop, it's pillar #4 and it's self-control and discipline. That's what you are lacking the most. You struggle with putting off what you want in the moment for what you want most. You struggle with delayed gratification and I am not sure you even know what you want most. As I mentioned earlier, all of these pillars tie together like a big Venn diagram and they are all interconnected. You get caught up in the day-to-day distractions because you don't have a focus on who you are or what you want and in the off chance that you do, you lack self-control and discipline it takes to navigate a world of distraction so you can stay on course with getting what you want."

Coach Kenny was right.

"Those people who know what they want are on a mission and while they are on the mission, they have self-control and discipline to stay on the course and the path that they set. They are not sucked into the temptations; they know the grass may be greener, plumper and plusher, but they stay the course."

"Like Odysseus who had his sailors tie him to the mast and put cotton and wax in their ears so that they could sail close to the song of the Sirens, yet not get so close that they got eaten by the demons posing as beautiful women of the seas, you must pre-commit and have the self-control and discipline to stay the course of your commitment.

"Matthew Simonds, how many pillars have we covered?" Coach Kenny asked.

"Man, we have hopped around some haven't we? Let me check my napkins. #1 Elite Mindset, #9 Leadership, #10 The Right Culture, #2 Motivation and Commitment, #3 Focus and Awareness, #5 Process Over Outcome and #4 Self-Control and Discipline. That makes seven. We have covered seven," I replied.

"Well, I have good news for you, son," Coach Kenny said gently as he reached over the table and squeezed my shoulders. "Pillar #4, Self-Control and Discipline is going to give you the exact steps to be able to go from red to green that fast," he declared as he snapped his fingers. "The world needs you to be a machine of green."

I was ready to get out of the red-light state I was living in and learn how to have the self-control and discipline to tap into the green-light state as often as possible.

I felt as if I understood the difference between a red-light and green-light state. I wanted to learn how to get into a green-light state and stay there.

"You recognize that if you are in a red-light state or a yellow light state you must have a release routine to get you back to green and back in control of yourself. That release routine follows a three-step process," Coach Kenny said. "You need to have (#1) a physical action that you make with an association that serves as a trigger for releasing the past and moving on to the next play or the next part of your day. You then (#2) take a deep releasing breath that you take looking at a fixed point we call a focal point to oxygenate your brain and get back in control of yourself. And then you (#3) have a verbal trigger you say that cuts off the past and cements your commitment to the present."

Coach Kenny then stood up, clapped his hands, took a deep breath, wiped his chest down with his hands as if he were wiping dirt off himself and said, '*GOOD. What's Important Now?*'

"That's been my release for years. I use it any time I get into a yellow or red light and it helps me to grow my self-control and discipline. I first need to have the awareness that I am in a yellow or red-light and then I have to have the self-control and discipline to let it go and get back to what's important now. Matthew Simonds, you also need to practice your release and anticipate that adversity is going to come so that you are not surprised. If you are surprised by adversity, there's the ego and the pride getting in the way again.

When you are surprised by adversity, you lack humility, you think it will be easy – and success is anything but easy, Matthew Simonds. You have to anticipate adversity and anticipate adrenaline when you get into critical moments of performance.

"Look, everything happens twice – first in your mind and then in reality. In order for you to become a machine of green, you must start by seeing yourself in a green-light state. You need to have a daily practice of mental imagery and meditation. Imagery to see yourself behaving how you want to behave and meditation to start building your ability to gain and then maintain self-control and stay present during the day."

"Do you have a current mental imagery and meditation practice Matthew Simonds?" Coach Kenny asked.

I didn't—and I didn't know where to start.

"Let me walk you through Pillar #6, mental imagery and meditation." Coach Kenny said.

CHAPTER 16
PILLAR #6
MENTAL IMAGERY AND MEDITATION

I felt like I had been in a rut for a while and meeting Coach Kenny was helping me to get out of that rut. I wanted more positivity and optimism in my life and was willing to pretty much try anything at this point. I had done mental imagery when I played high school football before games and Erin was big into meditation, but I wasn't doing either of those in my life.

"The strategies I use on a daily basis to help me be more positive, confident and prepared for a great day and create that green-light state are mental imagery and meditation," Coach Kenny said. "I will sit and close my eyes, and in my mind's eye I will imagine myself performing and my day unfolding exactly like I want it to. It's like watching a highlight video of my day before I live it.

"The Blue Angels, the Navy's best pilots that fly those amazing air shows, use imagery in preparation for their shows; and all the athletes I work with have a custom mental imagery audio that they listen to each day to help keep their minds right and see themselves performing how they want to perform. We record that on their phones using that same app that you are using to record our talk here, that voice memos app. We usually make it about 14:40 seconds long, as that is 1% of a day, and we call it our 1% mental performance mastery training tool."

"Coach Kenny, I have a question for you. Is mental imagery the same thing as visualization? We had a speaker come in and take our clients through visualization, and I have never been comfortable enough to do it on my own with them because I don't have a process or a framework to follow. Maybe that's because he was a speaker and not a MPM Coach. What you said about the difference between a speaker and a MPM Coach made so much sense to me. I have sat in on a lot of speakers who give you fluff and 'be positive' advice but not the strategies as to how to do it. How do I actually *do* mental imagery and meditation?" I asked.

"It's hard to teach others what we don't do ourselves. I actually think that's the definition of a hypocrite: asking others to do what you are not willing to do for yourself. It's why I don't like it when people call me a speaker and love it when they call me a MPM Coach. A MPM Coach is in the trenches with you. Speakers are going to have their one message, usually about their lives, and it's great for a short-term benefit – but what I do is legendary, not temporary. It's a long-term system and process, not a short-term fix, it's a system not a speech.

"Yes, mental imagery and visualization are the same thing. Mental imagery is different than just thinking about your job or performance. A lot of us daydream, and to a certain degree that can be productive. Daydreaming is when you quickly see yourself doing what you want to do or acting how you want to act, and it happens in a matter of seconds and is unscripted and unplanned. Speakers will tell you to do imagery, and a MPM Certified Coach will walk you through how to do mental imagery and will take you through it specific to your performance goals.

"Daydreaming about your performance happens in the shower, when sitting in class, etc. Mental imagery, on the other hand, is when you sit or lie down for three to thirty minutes and go through an exact routine for (#1) getting relaxed, (#2) affirming how you want to act or think, (#3) recalling your previous best performances, (#4) rehearsing for your next performance, and (#5) coming out of the relaxed state and coming back to the present. Mental imagery is structured, whereas daydreaming is not.

"The reason why imagery is effective is that the human brain cannot tell the difference between what you physically experience and what you vividly imagine. The brain processes them both with very similar psychoneuromuscular pathways, which in English means you have a physiological or a body response to a psychological or mental stimulus.

"You have experienced this. It's like when you are at a scary movie and a guy jumps out of a closet with an axe and you jump out of your seat," Coach Kenny said. "There is no danger to you, but your brain cannot tell the difference. Thus, you have a physiological/body response.

"The problem is that most people never tap into the power of structured mental imagery, and in the world of Mental Performance Mastery we believe that you never outperform your self-image and that everything happens twice – first in your mind, then in reality. If you want to strengthen your self-image, prepare for your competition and compete with more confidence, mental imagery is as good of a strategy for doing that as anything else."

I had not done any mental imagery or visualization since high school when Coach Allen would talk us through how we were going to play before we took the field. I used to love those sessions. I could actually feel myself throwing a touchdown, I could hear the crowd, I could smell the hot dogs that they grilled in the concession stand right behind our team bench. I could smell the amazing soups that they brought in from the world-famous 4-Acers Restaurant in our town and sold in small plastic football helmets. I could hear the cheerleaders with their BE AGGRESSIVE, B-E AGGRESSIVE, B-E-A-G-G-R-E-S-S-I-V-E, AGGRESSIVE, Got to BE AGRESSIVE cheer. Now I understood why he did that and why my boss brought in a speaker to tell us about mental imagery. Now I realized that my boss should have brought in a MPM coach to teach us how to take ourselves and our clients through mental imagery.

I wondered why I had not used mental imagery in my own life, with my clients, or with my kids? I wondered how much opportunity I had missed with them in Mental Performance Mastery. I needed and wanted to make a commitment to using mental imagery and meditation with my clients.

"Coach Kenny, I feel like you are giving me the keys to the kingdom of my future, yet I feel like there is so much for me to do to get caught up that I don't know where to start. How do I get it all done?" I asked.

"Well, Matthew Simonds, for the most part, you know what to do – you just are not doing what you know. Rome was not built in a day, and you will not get yourself out of the present situation you got yourself into over the last few years in a day either. It will take some time. Be patient, be present and be ok with not being perfect," Coach Kenny replied. *"The 10 Pillars of Mental Performance Mastery* is a lifestyle, not a magic bullet. Remember, what's built to last is not built fast, and one of the best and simplest ways to implement all of the pillars into your life on a consistent basis is to start strengthening your self-control and discipline as well as your focus and awareness with meditation. Let me teach you the basics of meditation.

"Close your eyes and inhale through your nose for a count of six, hold your breath for two and then exhale out of your mouth for a count of eight. Do that for five breaths."

As I sat there in the Protector Brewery and Burger, counting my breaths, I could feel myself becoming more present and could feel my mind and my heartrate slowing down.

"OK, that's five. How do you feel?" Coach Kenny asked.

"Wow. I feel more present and more under control," I responded.

"That's the goal of meditation. It's really that simple. Start with five breaths and work up to 10. The more you breathe and pause, the stronger your self-control and deeper your present-moment focus will become," Coach Kenny said. "Now, if you are going to do mental imagery, meditation or anything for that matter on a consistent basis, you must make that behavior a part of your daily routine – and that leads us to our next pillar, pillar #7."

CHAPTER 17
PILLAR #7
ROUTINES AND HABITS OF EXCELLENCE

"Routines and habits of excellence are critical because we become what we do on a daily basis. First, we make our habits, and then our habits make us," Coach Kenny continued. "Pillar #7 is about creating routines and habits of excellence."

Coach Kenny then reached for his iPhone and slid it across the table.

"Matthew Simonds. Do you like to fish?" he asked.

"I LOVE fishing. I hardly ever get to go," I replied as two of my favorite pictures I had hung up in my office came to mind. The first was a picture of Erin and me fly-fishing in Alaska, and the second was her holding a largemouth bass the size of her quad (and she was a hockey player) that she had caught with one of the best fishing guides in the world, the great Heath Autrey in Corsicana, Texas. It was the biggest bass I had ever seen, and she caught it... with a lot of help from Heath.

"Well, I love fishing as well," Coach Kenny stated. "And I love teaching a man to fish, more than catching him a fish.

"I want you to open up that app right there," he said, as he pointed to a green square with an elephant's head on it. "It's called Evernote. I live in that app. It's where I capture all of my thoughts so that I never lose them and so that I don't have to remember anything and can let the creative juices flow. It keeps me organized."

As I clicked on the Evernote App, up popped what looked like a library of three-ring binders. There was one for each of the 10 pillars, and there was one for what looked like each of Coach Kenny's clients.

"Click on that binder called *Pillar #7*," Coach Kenny suggested. "Then scroll down to the page that says, 'Poems and Quotes.'"

As I scrolled through what looked like Coach Kenny's library of research and life's work, I found the binder called *Pillar #7* and the note that said "Poems and Quotes."

"Is this it?" I asked as I showed him the screen.

"That's the one. I keep all of the content I find related to the 10 pillars in an Evernote folder under that pillars name. Go ahead and read that poem right there," Coach Kenny said.

I am your constant companion.

I am your greatest helper or your heaviest burden.

I will push you onward
or drag you down to failure.

I am completely at your command.

Half the things you do,
you might just as well turn over to me,
and I will be able to do them quickly and correctly.

I am easily managed;
you must merely be firm with me.

Show me exactly how you want something done,
and after a few lessons I will do it automatically.

I am the servant of all great men.

And, alas, of all failures as well.

Those who are great, I have made great.

Those who are failures, I have made failures.

*I am not a machine, though I work
with all the precision of a machine.*

Plus, the intelligence of a man.

*You may run me for profit, or run me for ruin;
it makes no difference to me.*

*Take me, train me, be firm with me
and I will put the world at your feet.*

Be easy with me, and I will destroy you.

Who am I?

I am a HABIT!

Author Unknown

"Wow! I need better habits," I said.

"We all do," Coach Kenny replied. "First we make our habits and then our habits make us. I used to think that we rose to the occasion and could flip a switch when the lights came on. Then I had a coach at one of our Olympic training camps say to me that as athletes, we don't rise to the occasion – we sink to our levels of training and habits. I thought that was so profound. That mindset about the importance of sinking to our levels of training and habits has stuck with me for over 50 years. Even as I say it today, I can clearly see the image of him saying that to us at the track in Oregon where we were training at the time.

"The key to having great habits is being able to have routines, and the key to having great routines is to have habits. My wife tells me that I am a machine of routine. She gets on me for setting an alarm clock each night because I have woken up before my alarm clock for the last 40+ years. I don't know if it even works because I turn it off before it would go off. My internal routine clock sure does though."

I couldn't remember the last time I woke up before my alarm clock. It might have been when Brina used to scream in her crib and Erin would go get her and the dogs would start barking and then my mind would start racing and I would get up, make a pot of black coffee and start checking e-mail. The only routine I had in my life was swiping my phone screen to snooze and trying to sleep as long as possible, putting off what had to be done that day. Another example of my lack of self-control and discipline and my lack of routines and habits of excellence.

"Matthew Simonds, the secrets of success are hidden in the routines of our daily life," Coach Kenny stated. "The golfers I work with know all about routine. The kickers I work with in the PFL know all about routine. The real estate agents I work with know all about routine. It's one of life's great secrets that you become what you do on a daily basis. But it's no longer a secret for you, Matthew Simonds, because I just told you."

"You are so right, Coach Kenny." I chuckled at his joke about one of life's great secrets no longer being a secret. "I feel like you are telling me all of life's great secrets. Meeting you has been amazing."

"Thank you for your kind words, Matthew Simonds," Coach Kenny said. "But let me ask you this. How much of what we have talked about have you ever heard before?"

As I sat back and thought about it, I realized that I had heard almost all of what Coach Kenny was saying at various points in my life; I had just never heard it all put into such an easy and organized system as *The 10 Pillars of Mental Performance Mastery*. And I hadn't implemented it because I needed a coach to guide me. I was told, not taught, about the various aspects of *The 10 Pillars of Mental Performance Mastery* over the course of my career. I had heard a lot of speakers and not been given much system.

"Almost all of it," I answered.

"You are like most people," Coach Kenny said. "And we call that average. Like I have said, I hate the word *average*. It means you are the best of the worst and the worst of the best. It's a terrible place to live.

"You know what to do; you just don't do what you know because you don't have an elite mindset, you lack leadership, and you have not surrounded yourself with the right culture. You also lack motivation and commitment and don't have the focus and awareness that you need to achieve. Your process is working great for the outcomes you are getting, and those outcomes you are getting are not the outcomes you are wanting. Your self-control and discipline are weak, you don't' understand delayed gratification and the greatness that comes with putting off what you want in the moment for what you want most and you can't imagine the future you want because you don't visualize, meditate or create the quiet space you need in your daily routine to do so. You don't have an accountability partner or a mentor to help you grow either. You are slowly dying on an island of isolation – merely existing, not living and growing. You are giving the world your B or C game and you don't even know it because you have never been trained on how to give you're A game."

I was starting to feel about as small as one of the sesame seeds on top of the hamburger bun I had eaten earlier.

"Oh, now – don't cower up because I am coaching you hard. I am coaching you hard because I care. When you cower up, that's not elite, that's selfish because you think about how you are feeling and not about the gifts you are being given by someone who cares. Get out of your feelings and face the facts. Be coachable, take constructive criticism and feedback as a compliment and say *thank you*. Look, the beautiful part of you falling short in all of those areas, Matthew Simonds, is that we can fix all of them. It's about decisions, behaviors, awareness, commitments and scheduling," Coach Kenny said, filling up my tires with the air of hope. "Once we get you an a.m. and p.m. routine, you will slowly start taking over control of your life and living with intention and on the path of living the life you want to live. I will be your accountability partner and mentor you in my MPM system. I am here to help you along the way. But if we are going to create a great daily routine, it's only going to get executed if you have pillar #8. Without pillar #8 you will go through the motions rather than *grow* through the motions."

CHAPTER 18
PILLAR #8
TIME MANAGEMENT & ORGANIZATION

"Do you know what the only factor that every Olympic athlete, every corporate executive and every person in this airport right now has in common?" Coach Kenny asked.

"That we are all winners and learners?" I said.

"Very good," Coach Kenny said. "I see you workin', – but no. That's not what I meant."

"I have no idea," I responded with a smile.

"Time. Time is the ONLY factor that is the same for everyone on the planet. Time is the ONLY factor that is the same for every Olympic athlete, every corporate executive that wants the big contract, and for every high school football player and coach that wants to win on Friday night," Coach Kenny declared.

"We are all given 86,400 seconds and 1,440 minutes in a day and 168 hours in a week. No more. No less. How we choose to spend or invest that time will dictate almost everything in our lives.

"When I was training for the Olympics, I had a coach say to me one time: *Kenny, if you had a bank account that credited you with $86,400 every day and you were not allowed to take any money with you to the next day, and no matter how much you spent or how much you kept the next day you had $86,400 in your account, what would you do?*

"I told him that I would either spend it all, give it all away or do something productive with it because the next day I would have $86,400 dollars again. What would you do with a bank account like that, Matthew Simonds?"

As I thought about it, the first thing that came to my mind was the #1 goal I had: to achieve financial security by paying off my house, eliminating any debt, having a strong financial safety net and living off interest.

"I think I would retire and spend as much time with Erin, Brina and Michael as I could," I said.

"Well, the first thing you must do is eliminate the word *spend* from your vocabulary and insert the word *invest* – that's part of the elite mindset and also part of knowing that your time here in this game called life is limited. Time is the one thing we can't get back and we can't' get more of. Matthew Simonds, you know you do have that bank account with $86,400. It's called life, and you are given 86,400 seconds a day to invest or spend; it's up to you," Coach Kenny stated. "My next question is, do you know where your time is going? Are you in control of your time or is your time in control of you?"

As I finished my torrid pace of note taking on another napkin, I sat back and thought for a minute. Did I have any clue how much of my time every day was going towards my work vs. my family, my wealth vs. my health? I had no idea.

"Coach Kenny, I have always struggled with time management and organization. I always try to get more done than I give myself time for and I end up getting stressed out and don't create the highest quality of work. I don't think any of my clients know the difference, but I do."

"If you know that you are not giving your very best, your clients do as well," Coach Kenny said. "If you are going to sign your name to something, it better be your best work. Things that are built to last are not built fast, and we must keep our focus on doing work that is legendary and here forever vs. temporary and here today, gone tomorrow."

Things that are built to last are not built fast. Do work that is legendary, not temporary. I had heard these before. These were two of the motivational messages that Coach Allen had hung up in our locker room 20 years ago. He called them signs of success (SOS), and at the end of each season I would ask him for photocopies and hang them up in my room at home. It was a great way to advertise and conditioning the mindset that I wanted.

He had a couple others that I remembered from one of his good friends and one of the top lacrosse coaches in the country, Morgan Randall: *How you do anything is how you do everything. Excellence in small things is excellence in all things.* Coach Randall was later featured in a book entitled *Seeds of Success* by MPM Certified Coach John Brubaker, which had become one of my favorite reads.

Coach Kenny continued. "Time is a constant and is always ticking. We never know how much time we have left and we want to be sure we are taking as much control of our time as possible. You must create a system for how you map out your time, and I have an acronym for *system* I want to teach you:

S.Y.S.T.E.M.

Save

Yourself

Stress

Time

Effort

Money & Motivation

"I have a system where I sit down each Sunday night and map out my 168 hours for the week. I map out for each day when I am going to do. I map out the week loosely, sometimes two weeks in advance and then get really detailed for my next day, the ultimate microscope – the next day. I always get detailed with scheduling tomorrow tonight before I go to bed as part of my p.m. routine. On that schedule I will list out:

1. Go to sleep and wake up
2. Eat and meal prep for the week

3. Do my recovery workouts like go to physical therapy, take an ice bath, do yoga, or get a massage
4. Lift weights, exercise, and do conditioning
5. Do my mental imagery and meditation
6. Do recreational sports like golf, tennis and walking
7. Read and do my professional development
8. Get ready, shower, dress, brush my teeth, do laundry, etc.
9. Do transportation time such as driving or flying
10. Social time with my wife, friends, kids and grandkids
11. And my time for observing faith

"I map all of that out for the week on Sunday and then each night I look at my plan for the next day and see if that's still how I want to attack my day, drill it down in more detail and really focus on planning tomorrow today. Here, take a look."

Coach Kenny handed me back his cell phone and showed me how he mapped out his day in a Google Doc on his phone. He said that he actually created it on his computer and then would maintain or update it on his phone as necessary. I was blown away at the detail he put into his plan for the week.

"Have you always mapped out your time like this?" I asked.

"I have for about the last 50 years. We had a coach with the Olympics that stressed to us that being an Olympic champion was a lifestyle, not an event, and that winning a medal didn't happen by accident, that it happened by intention and the first place to get uber intentional was with your time. It happened by setting a target, mapping out a course and a plan of action, and then following it. This really struck a chord with me. I then met with him weekly until I learned to master his 168-plan technique. I used to do this in paper and pencil and now I do it on my computer in Google Docs and update it in the Google Docs app on my phone.

"It took me a while to change, but I had to stay up on the technology or I was going to get passed by," Coach Kenny said with pride. "I am a competitor and I was not going to let that happen. I won't be beat because of technology. I may be old, but I am on it. Heck, I can even do the Ninja celebration dance from *Fortnite*," Coach Kenny said as he got up and danced by the table.

I was totally blown away by his attention to detail and the intentionality in which he planned his days. He had scheduled time for sending a text to his wife in the morning and for FTK-ing her at night. I had nothing like that on my schedule because I did not keep one written out; it was all in my head.

"Coach Kenny, this is awesome!" I exclaimed. "But I sort of feel like I am trying to drink from a fire hydrant right now. Where do I get started?"

"Matthew Simonds, remember, it's the start that stops most people, and you are in the total immersion learning stage. You ARE drinking from the fire hydrant. It's supposed to be like that. We will get you started. But before we get you started on your journey into the *10 Pillars of Mental Performance Mastery*, we should probably get the check and get out of here before they turn the lights off on us."

As I looked around, there was NOBODY else left in the Protector Brewery and Burger. I looked down at my watch and we had been sitting there for north of four hours. It was almost 11 o'clock at night.

CHAPTER 19
THE CHECK AND THE WALK

Lynn, the waitress, came over and gave us our check. I grabbed it first and Coach Kenny quickly put his hand on top of mine.

"I told you earlier that I was not taking any new clients and that I was buying this dinner," he said. "Don't deny me the pleasure I will receive from buying you dinner, Matthew Simonds."

"Coach Kenny, please. Let me get this," I said.

"Your money is no good here," Coach Kenny replied. "One of my friends owns this Protector Brewery and Burger. I got this."

He took out a crisp $100 bill and wrote a message on it: *For the lovely Lynn. Thank you for your service. Keep smiling.* He then put the $100 bill under the check.

We got up and started walking out of the restaurant, but not before I could glimpse down at the bill and saw that it was for zero dollars.

"Coach Kenny, were those burgers and drinks for free?" I asked. "Why was the bill for zero dollars?"

"No, they cost the owner of the restaurant what they cost financially to produce. They cost the chef the time to make them; Lynn the time to bring them to us; the farmer who grew the mushrooms, onion and peppers the time to grow them; the farmer who cut the grain the time to grow it; the baker that made the buns the time to bake them; and above all else, the cows who provided the milk for the cheese and the meat for the burger the time to produce the milk, and it also cost one of those cows their lives. You could say the cows were truly committed to the hamburger. There's a lot more that goes into making great hamburgers than we think," Coach Kenny said. "We take for granted the simple things like being able to get a hamburger that tastes that good as easily as walking up to the counter and ordering."

"That's a great point. I never thought of that. Pretty amazing all that goes into a hamburger and all that we take for granted," I replied. "I noticed on the bill that there was a zero balance and you left a $100 bill."

"I gave Lynn my credit card when you went to the bathroom and told her to NOT let you pay for this," Coach Kenny said as we started walking out of the restaurant. "That $100 was for her service. She was great. And that note I left her. That's a part of my routine. If I can do anything to help make someone's day a little bit brighter, I do it. It takes no skill to be positive and to help brighten up someone's day and put them into a green-light state."

As we started walking down the terminal, following signs towards the airport hotel, I wanted to know how to get out of the red-light state I was in and back into a green-light state as fast as possible.

I knew that Lynn would go green when she got her $100 tip, and Coach Kenny was in green from giving it to her. I still felt red from thinking about how far I had drifted off course since that great night on the cruise shaking it to DJ Gulian and how I was going to get home ASAP.

"You know, Matthew Simonds," Coach Kenny commented, "the most challenging and rewarding part of *The 10 Pillars of Mental Performance Mastery* is growth and progress. Progress is the goal. I feel like you made some progress in moving from the red-light state you were in earlier towards the green-light state that you are in now. Could you feel the difference when I had you stand up just a few minutes ago and go green and then go red?"

"I sure could – it was crazy," I said. "I think I might be in a yellow light, though, Coach Kenny. I just need to get back home."

"You will when you do. It's out of your control at this point. I could see you shift from red to green throughout our time together," Coach Kenny replied. "Now that you have an idea of what it means to recognize your signal lights, the next step is to master your ability to release and refocus, to get distracted, recognize it and then get back to the present and your process so you can be productive. You have to be able to let go of the negative so that you can grow the positive. Let the negative go and let the positive grow."

"That makes sense, Coach Kenny," I said. "But how do you do it? I hear people say you have to be positive all the time, but that's easier said than done."

"The first step is to recognize that you are in a red-light state. Once you do that, you go through the release routine and 'flush it,'" Coach Kenny said, making a movement with his hand of flushing a toilet.

"Like when you had me go to the bathroom to flush away the napkin with all of the things I could not control on it?" I asked.

"That's exactly it. The physical act of flushing the toilet is a release. The physical act of doing something to associate with flushing it is exactly what a release is. It might be clapping your hands like I showed you earlier, crumpling up a piece of paper and throwing it away, making a fist or tightening a part of your body and then letting it go or stomping your feet, but do something to let it go and flush it."

"Brina is good at that. She stomps her feet all the time when she is in red lights," I said, laughing as I thought about my little girl stomping away in frustration.

"You know what, though? She is amazing. She will always come skipping back seconds later with another request and a huge smile on her face. She can go from red to green that fast," I said as I snapped my fingers.

"Sounds like she has a good release already," Coach Kenny said. "Most of us have a physical release that we do naturally, but because we don't have the awareness and an association that what we physically do is our release of that red light and negative energy, we are inconsistent with it and It doesn't have the cleansing effect of getting us back to green or back to a yellow from a red that we want it to have.

"After we release, we have to refocus and one of the best ways to refocus is to talk to yourself, not listen to yourself. When we are in red lights, we listen to ourselves. We listen to ourselves about how bad our situation is, how we feel or how unfair life is, etc., and we can get back to green lights by talking to ourselves."

I was a little confused. I did not know the difference between talking to and listening to myself.

"When you get into red lights, think of a little character dressed in red we call the red assassin or Debbie Downer. This character tells you how you are no good, how you got cheated, how you should quit, that it's not worth it or not fair, etc.

When you listen to that negative voice, you are listening to yourself.

"On the other shoulder is a character dressed in green that we call the green assassin, Positive Paula. This character speaks to you with the voice of reason, talking to you about what's important now, about what you can do positively and constructively to improve your position in this moment, about what you can control," Coach Kenny explained. "When you talk to yourself, it's this voice speaking. When you talk to yourself, you can refocus back to the moment.

"When you listen to yourself, you get stuck in the past or projected into the future, and in either place you will drown in a sea of negativity. When you talk to yourself, you can do anything," Coach Kenny stated.

"So when we listen to ourselves, it's negative and when we talk to ourselves, it's positive?" I asked for clarification.

"That's about right," Coach Kenny answered. "Look, everyone has their own ways of using their focus and awareness to recognize their signal lights, to then release the red and yellow and refocus on what's important now in a green-light mentality. The simplest way I can teach awareness and self-control is through using the signal lights.

"When you recognize red lights, you want to have a physical release to flush your red lights and then talk yourself back into green lights using a trigger word or phrase like *right here, right now*."

Just as Coach Kenny had finished saying *right here, right now*, we were in the lobby at the airport hotel.

I wanted more of *The 10 Pillars of Mental Performance Mastery.* I was not ready for this journey to be over.

CHAPTER 20
THE HOTEL LOBBY

"Well, Coach Kenny, looks like this might be the end of the road?" I said as we walked up to the hotel front desk.

"Never the end of the road, Matthew Simonds; always a bend in the road," Coach Kenny said. "I told you I was not taking on any more clients... because I don't have any."

"What do you mean, you don't have any clients?" I asked. "The guy that owned the Protector Brewery and Burger? The MMA world champion that fell through the trampoline you were on the phone with earlier, all the football coaches– aren't those guys your clients?"

"I don't think of them as clients. I think of them as friends, remember?" Coach Kenny said. "I was an individual-sport athlete and had only a few close teammates when I was younger. I missed out on that team experience, and as I evolved, I realized the power of friends, family and teammates. *Team* might be the most powerful word in the world – more powerful than *family* because family is by birth and team is by choice, and there is nothing stronger than human choice.

People are not born into the military; they choose to go and fight and that's why the SEAL teams are so strong. They are created by choice, and they have a strong connection from the time and shared adversity they have all had together. I see myself as a teammate and friend to the people in my life that most people would call clients. I am not taking any more clients, but I would be honored to be your friend and teammate."

I loved that perspective: Treat your clients like friends, family and teammates. *Team* is the most powerful word in the world. The concept of team and friends was genius. And team, family and friends were missing from my life.

"Coach Kenny, I don't only want you to be my friend and on my team. I need you to be my friend, mentor and coach. Tonight has been life changing. I am going to put *The 10 Pillars of Mental Performance Mastery* into use immediately, and I want to get certified." I said. "Boy, am I glad I sat next to you on the plane! What was one of the worst things that could happen to me today has turned out to be one of the best."

"That too, Matthew Simonds, is a part of the elite mindset," Coach Kenny responded. "Turn the worst things that happen to you into the best things that have happened to you."

"This is one layover I will remember for the rest of my life. Please, let me get you a room here at this airport hotel," I said. "I have so many points from traveling that I can get us each a room for free."

Then I heard a voice from behind the desk…

CHAPTER 21
SOLD OUT

"Next in line. Excuse me, sir. Sir."

I walked to the front desk and approached the woman who was speaking. She was the general manager of the airport hotel.

"I hate to say this, but we are all sold out tonight. We have no rooms available," she said.

"No rooms available!" I said in frustration as I threw my hands in the air. "You have to be kidding me. Can you call any of your other properties in the area and see if they have any rooms available?"

"I am so sorry, sir," the woman replied. "We have been turning people away all night and have called every hotel within an hour's drive, and they are all sold out as well. With tomorrow being Thanksgiving and with the undefeated Detroit Dominators playing at home against the Chicago Beez in the Professional Football League, coupled with the Detroit Triathlon on Friday, it seems like everyone from all over the world is in Detroit at the same time. I'm so sorry."

As I clapped my hands hard, wiped my shirt and took a big deep breath to release, I turned around to see what Coach Kenny wanted to do.

But Coach Kenny was nowhere to be seen.

I had no idea where he went – he was just there a minute ago.

There I was.

Standing at the airport hotel counter in the Detroit airport.

Alone.

I didn't know what I was going to do or where Coach Kenny had gone.

All I knew was I needed to find a way to get home and start applying *The 10 Pillars of Mental Performance Mastery* before it was too late.

CHAPTER 22
ALONE AT THE COUNTER

"Do you know where the rental car facility is?" I asked the woman at the hotel front desk who had broken the bad news to me that there was no availability at their hotel—or within an hour of the airport. Now that Coach Kenny had disappeared, I was planning to rent a car and start my drive back to Paradise Valley, Arizona, all 18+ hours. I also thought it was weird that he would just disappear like that.

"Sir, we have called over to the rental car facility as well and they are all sold out. They are working on getting some cars here from Chicago. With Thanksgiving tomorrow and the big football game and triathlon, they told me that they don't think they will have any cars here till Saturday at the earliest," the woman said with empathy in her voice. "I am so sorry. I wish I could be of more help to you. This has never happened before. Detroit has never been this busy."

I was exhausted, alone, and had no idea what I was going to do. There were no rental cars available, no hotel rooms available and the next flight back to Arizona wasn't till Saturday morning, two days after Thanksgiving and one day after my wife Erin's birthday. I picked up the phone to call her and deliver more bad news.

CHAPTER 23
THE PHONE CALL HOME

"Well, that's just perfect, Matthew Simonds, just perfect," Erin said through her tears as I explained how I was not going to be making it home till Saturday.

"Erin, I tried," I explained. "The rental car facility is sold out and the hotel is sold out. I was going to drive home and now I have nowhere to go. I don't even know what to do."

"Matthew, you'll figure it out," Erin said. "I took the next four days off from work so we could spend some time together as a family and now you aren't even going to be here. I am tired of this, Matthew Simonds. Really tired of it."

As the conversation came to a close, I felt a lump in my throat. I was trying to get home and couldn't. What was I going to do?

As I started to walk back into the terminal to find a place to sit down and try to figure it all out, I heard a familiar voice calling my name.

"Matthew Simonds. Hey, Matthew Simonds..."

CHAPTER 24
THE VOICE

The voice belonged to Coach Kenny.

"Hey, sorry about that. I had to go to the bathroom and couldn't wait any longer. It just hit me. And at my age, when the bathroom calls... you answer," Coach Kenny said with a chuckle.

"Man, am I sure glad to see you!" I said with a glimmer of hope that I was no longer alone. "The hotel is all sold out, there are no rooms available within an hour's drive of here, and there are no rental cars available either."

"GOOD!" Coach Kenny exclaimed. "More time for us to keep talking and for me to share with you *The 10 Pillars of Mental Performance Mastery*. When life throws you a lemon, you can get sour or you can make lemonade. Let me make a couple calls."

As Coach Kenny started flipping through his phone, I took out my phone and texted to myself, *When life throws you a lemon, you can get sour or make lemonade.* Coach Kenny was truly a mental performance master one of the most positive people I had ever met. It seemed like the more adverse the situation got, the more energy and focus he had. He didn't have time for negativity, pity and sorrow.

I excused myself and went to the restroom. As I was walking out, Coach Kenny was on the phone and motioning to me to come over towards him. He hung up just as I was getting there.

"How ironic is this?" he said. "Remember our waitress Lynn? She was so floored by the note on the bill we left her that she called Sean, my former Navy SEAL friend that owns that Protector Brewery and Burger. He called me as I was getting ready to call him. I literally had his contact open. He lives here, is in town for the holiday and is actually on his way here, to the airport, to pick up some of his former Navy SEAL teammates who are in town to participate in the Detroit Triathlon on Friday.

"He said we could crash at his place if you wanted to. You will love him – he lives the 10 pillars and has as much of an elite mindset as anyone I have ever met and is as open to teaching how he thinks, what he believes and how he lives his life. Sometimes people don't talk about how they live their life because they are too concerned that people will judge them. Sean doesn't care what other people say or what other people think. He is only focused on being the best version of himself that he can be for himself, his family and his country and has no pride and no ego. He is totally focused on progress. I think you should come."

At this point I had no other options and the opportunity to spend more time with Coach Kenny was something that I couldn't say *no* to. I wasn't someone who normally would stay in a house with people I didn't know, yet I was pretty excited about meeting Sean and getting more time with Coach Kenny.

CHAPTER 25
MEETING SEAN

As we walked out of the terminal to Passenger Pick-up, there was a group of four guys standing together that had a presence to them like they were elite and tough as nails. This had to be Sean's group of SEAL teammates that were in town for the Triathlon.

"Excuse me. Are you guys getting picked up by Sean?" Coach Kenny asked as he walked confidently over to the group being as proactive as one can be.

"Yes, we are, sir. How did you know that?" asked one of the SEALs.

"Oh, great. Sean and I go way back," Coach Kenny said as he extended his hand to shake hands with the men. "He said he was on his way here to pick up four of his former teammates and you guys look like you fit the bill. I am Kenneth John Henry Johnson; my friends call me Coach Kenny."

"Coach Kenny, it's nice to meet you. I am David, and this is Chris, Adam and Kyle. We are in town for the Detroit Triathlon on Friday, here to see

Sean, and were hoping to catch the Dominators and Beez game tomorrow but it's sold out. I don't know the last time they were both undefeated this late into the season," David explained.

"This is my friend Matthew Simonds. We just met tonight in the airport, but I feel like I have known him forever," Coach Kenny said with a smile as I extended my hand to shake those of the four men.

"Nice to meet you guys," I said.

"How do you guys know Sean?" one of the SEALs asked.

"I worked with him when he was a football player in college. I was the teams' Mental Performance Mastery coach," Coach Kenny answered. "As the captain of the team, Sean was in my office more than any other player."

"I bet he was," David said. "Sean is the most mentally tough human being I have ever been around. He has the most elite mindset of anyone I have ever met. I am sure he would have eaten up Mental Performance Mastery training. Now that you mention it, he used to talk about a guy he worked with when he was in college; the guy used to be an Olympian. Sean always talked about how he was juiced up all the time and full of energy. Are you that guy?"

"That's me," Coach Kenny said with a smile.

"Man, small world. It's so nice to meet you," David replied.

"Hey guys, remember that Mental Performance Mastery coach Sean had in college that he always talked about when we were prepping for missions overseas?" David turned to ask the three other men. "Well, this is the guy. This is Coach Kenny. What a small world!"

A small world it was. And I was glad to have met Coach Kenny when I did. He seemed to know everyone.

Just then a black Escalade with tinted windows and black rims pulled up, and out hopped a man who immediately ran over and gave Coach Kenny a hug and embraced each of the four SEALs.

"Sean, I want you to meet Matthew Simonds," Coach Kenny said as he introduced the two of us.

I held out my hand to shake hands with Sean and he came right in and gave me a hug. It felt like I was getting hugged by a bear. Sean was in phenomenal shape.

"Any friend of Coach Kenny is a friend of mine," Sean said. "It's great to meet you, Matthew Simonds. Glad you can come and spend the night."

As we all piled into the Escalade, I felt like I was in the presence of the elite. I was in the presence of men who had served our country and were highly trained both physically and mentally. I was intimidated and excited at the same time. I always had a fascination with Navy SEALs, their elite mindset and culture within the teams, but I had never met a SEAL in person.

As we drove back to Sean's house, I sat quietly in the back listening to the men share stories and updates on their wives and children. I could feel the love they had for their families.

As we approached what had to be Sean's house, high in the hills overlooking the city, I was finally getting tired and wanting to go to bed, as it was just a tick after 1am now on Thursday, Thanksgiving Day. It had been a long day.

I was hoping to get up early and see if there was any shot of getting a rental car or on another flight back to the desert of Arizona to catch up to Erin, Brina and Michael.

CHAPTER 26
SEAN'S HOUSE

When we got to Sean's house, he opened the front door and we walked into the main room of the house. It was beautiful.

A floor-to-ceiling stone fireplace had to be 14 feet tall. A wall of windows overlooked a small lake that you could only see because the moon was so bright. The crackling of the fire in the fireplace and his two black French Bulldogs that reminded me of Yotie and Cypress were lying down quietly in their beds by the fireplace, making the house seem very homey.

I wish Yotie and Cypress did that. We had paid for them to get trained but never followed up on the training that we were to do when we got home. As I learned, dog training is really dog owner training, especially when you have twin French Bulldog princesses.

Sean showed me to the guest room where I would be staying. It was upstairs overlooking the main room. Inside the room on the wall were beautiful mounted deer, ducks and largemouth bass and pictures of Sean and his friends at the best golf courses in the world. I had dreamed of having a room like that one day. I guess to have those you actually had to hunt, fish and play golf and to hunt, fish and play golf you had to make the time to do so.

"Did you catch all of these?" I asked.

"Sure did," Sean replied. "My wife actually got that deer and we each got one of the ducks. Do you hunt or fish?"

"Sean, I love to fish but I have never hunted," I said. "Sad to say, I have never shot a gun. Nothing against it; I actually want to start hunting. A lot of my friends back in Arizona do it. I just seem to always be working when they are hunting or playing golf."

"There is nothing like it, Matthew Simonds," Sean stated with a huge smile. "Sitting out there in a tree stand or in a duck blind before the sun comes up or floating on a bass boat or making contact with a golf ball with your club face. The peace and quiet, the chase – it's part of what makes me love hunting and golf so much. I also just love the art of shooting whether it's a gun or a golf ball; it's totally a mental game. I'll have to take you sometime. But for now, get some rest. Sleep fast and I will see you in the morning."

As Sean walked out of the room and shut the door behind him, I felt like I was with my former high school football teammates. Coach Kenny, Sean, Chris, David, Kyle and Adam reminded me of my best friends from the team. They were all in great shape, positive, motivated and seemed to have it all together. I was inspired by their presence.

Coach Allen used to always tell us that you became the average of the five people you hung out with most and the average of the five habits you executed daily, and these were the types of guys that I wish I got more time with on a consistent basis. Iron sharpens iron and I was a feather compared to these guys.

Come to think of it, the only people I hung out with were the people I worked with, and I was traveling so much that I only saw them a few times a year each. I was craving for a core group of friends and the bond that these guys had.

CHAPTER 27
RISE AND GRIND

Knock, knock, knock.

As I jumped up in bed like the Undertaker sitting up in the center of the ring in a WWE match, I looked at my watch. It was 5:00am. I had for sure slept fast.

"Matthew Simonds," a voice from outside the door said.

Knock, knock, knock.

I got out of bed and opened the door.

"Hey, did I wake you?" Coach Kenny asked, covered in sweat wearing gym shorts and a t-shirt. "We just finished a run and were going to do a yoga session by the fireplace. I figured you would want to sleep in and were probably not much of a runner, but wanted to see if you would join us for yoga? I remember you saying your wife did yoga and you were wanting to get started, so here is your opportunity to take a step into being the next and best version of you."

"She does – good memory," I said. "I am not much of a yoga guy. Why are you guys up so early?"

"Matthew Simonds, welcome to the 5am Club, the club that anyone can join by choice, but most don't because of comfort," Coach Kenny said. "A key to success is to get up while the clock still reads 5am, before the clock strikes 6am, to get comfortable with being uncomfortable, and to act differently than how you feel. That's a big part of why we run in the morning and part of why we are doing yoga now. You may not be much of a yoga guy, well, today you are, my friend! Come on; here is a pair of shorts and a t-shirt. Meet us down by the fireplace in five minutes," Coach Kenny urged as he walked off.

Erin was always asking me to go to a yoga class or do yoga with her and the kids at the house. I was yet to do either. Now I was going to do a class with guys I hardly knew? I was going to embarrass myself. I wasn't even close to being in as good of shape as these guys were, but I wasn't about to be disrespectful and go back to bed. What was I getting myself into?

I changed my clothes and walked downstairs to the fireplace. As I walked in, Sean looked at me with a smile and said, "Rise and grind, Matthew Simonds. Rise and Grind to Get Some, Thanks for joining us."

"Welcome to the 5am Club, the club of champions," said David, who was wearing no shirt and had the Navy SEAL trident tattooed on his absolutely ripped chest.

"Rise and grind, Matthew Simonds. Shall we get started, men?" Chris asked. "Kyle, let's do an easier flow this morning. We don't want to be too hard on Matthew Simonds and we also have to do that race tomorrow. No crazy stuff, man."

"Have to, Chris?" Kyle said as he looked Chris in the eye. "We get to do that triathlon, bro. We get to, never have to. Get your mind right."

"Hooyah, Kyle," Chris responded. "Get to! Get to Get Some. Give Everything Today…"

"So Others May Excel" – The group of SEALs shouted back in unison as they chuckled recalling the Get Some mindset they all learned about in hell week.
As I stepped onto a towel between Coach Kenny and Sean, in front of the fireplace, Kyle started to lead us through some breathing exercises.

I felt uneasy, uncomfortable and out of place. Little did I know, that's exactly how I was supposed to feel. I was about to get comfortable with being uncomfortable and was going to have to act differently than how I felt.

Welcome to the 5am Club.

CHAPTER 28
NAMASTE

"Namaste," Kyle said as we all sat with our legs crossed and hands together at our chest in a prayer position.

"Namaste," we all repeated in unison.

As our yoga session came to a close, I had never felt more alive, more present and more connected to the moment than I did in that moment. Erin had always talked about the physical and mental benefits of yoga and I had always laughed. I was a former football player; I was into weights, actually to be honest I was into nothing physical including yoga. Until now.

"That was awesome!" I said. "Thanks for teaching us, Kyle, and thanks for getting me up out of bed, Coach Kenny. That was the first time I have ever done yoga. I loved it."

"Yoga is my preferred type of exercise," Coach Kenny replied. "You gain core strength, flexibility and mindfulness. You don't pound your joints like you do when you run and you can do it anywhere; you don't need to go to a gym. I've been practicing ever since I started working with Special Operations Warriors and MMA fighters. They do yoga all the time and now it's as mainstream in sports training as lifting weights. PFL teams, pro golfers – they all do yoga."

I loved it. I wondered why I had waited so long to try it. The best part about it was that I could do yoga with Erin and it would be doing two things at once – fitness training and getting time with her.

"Hey, Matthew Simonds, you drink black coffee?" Sean asked.

"Sure do," I answered, although I felt like I needed water more than coffee – I had sweat a ton.

Sean came back into the main room with a coffee pot and mugs for us all. As he poured me a cup, the other guys started to sit in a circle by the fireplace.

"Matthew Simonds, come on over here," Coach Kenny said as he slapped his hand on the chair to his left, motioning for me to sit next to him.

As I sat down and sipped my black coffee, Sean thanked each of the guys for being a part of his life: "Guys, I love you all. If it weren't for you guys, I am not sure I would have lived through some of those missions."

"Hooyah, Sean," David replied.

"Coach Kenny, I want to thank you for teaching me about what it takes to have an elite mindset back when we worked together while I was in college. I have used those same 10 pillars of mental performance mastery you taught us in football for the rest of my life. Whether in college football, on a mission as a SEAL, leading a platoon, leading my family or running Protector Brewery and Burgers all over the country, having an elite mindset has helped me the entire way," Sean said.

"Matthew Simonds, it's such a blessing that you are with us today. I know you got stuck in travel and are trying to get home to your wife and kids for the holiday. If you are going to be here with us, I would love to share with you some depth on pillar #1 elite mindset that Coach Kenny taught me all those years ago and that I still use today. He told me that you were looking to take your life to the next level, and I can tell you that growing and elite mindset and using *The 10 Pillars of Mental Performance Mastery* have not only changed my life but those of my teammates here as well."

Chris, David, Kyle and Adam all nodded their heads.

"Hooyah, Sean," Adam agreed. "The 10 pillars saved my life on more than one occasion. They are a big part of why I am still here today. They helped me through some dark times, man."

"Sean, Coach Kenny introduced me to *The 10 Pillars of Mental Performance Mastery* yesterday," I said. "I would love to hear about how you guys train your elite mindset. Do you have a notebook or napkins that I can use to take notes?"

Coach Kenny laughed and told the others about how I had taken notes on napkins while we were talking in the airport Protector Brewery and Burger. *The 10 Pillars of Mental Performance Mastery* were so good that I could hardly wait to hear more in-depth about how these warriors train an elite mindset.

CHAPTER 29
3 BLOCKS IN THE FOUNDATION

As Sean went to get a notebook for me, I went back to my room to get my phone. I was going to record this session as well so that I could come back to this just like I would *The 10 Pillars of Mental Performance Mastery* sessions with Coach Kenny at Protector Brewery and Burger.

When I returned to the main room, everyone was sitting in a circle and they all had laptops with a Google Doc open to take notes on. I took a seat in my chair between Sean and Coach Kenny.

"All right, men," Sean said with the stern and strong voice you would expect from a SEAL Team leader. "Remember, you train an elIte mindset just like you train your body or any other physical skill. You must first master the three blocks in the foundation of training an elite mindset – the three blocks that make the foundation from which we build our elite mindset.

"(#1) We want to have a total immersion experience followed by (#2) spaced repetition.

That spaced repetition is what we call doing a little, a lot.

"That's why they have us go through boot camp and why most businesses have a week-long training process you go through when you get hired. You go through a total immersion learning experience, like going through a certification course in strength and conditioning or in Mental Performance Mastery. You then have to back that up with spaced repetitious follow-up and mentorship to keep sharpening your skills.

"The training... That's one of the things I have missed most about retiring from the SEAL Teams, the total immersion of training for a mission and the spaced repetition trainings between missions. Man, I miss the training."

"Hooyah, Sean," Adam said. "I remember you talking about the importance of a total immersion experience followed by spaced repetition when we were in boot camp and you were our leader. What was the third part to training the foundation you were so passionate about?"

"Thanks for getting me back on track, Adam," Sean replied. "The third block in the foundation (#3) is having an accountability partner and a support person who can help hold you accountable to your process and also having a mentor and coach who will show you the way, speed up your learning curve and help you avoid the mistakes that they had made.

"Having a coach or mentor that you report to on your progress so that you are assured to *grow* through the motions and not just go through the motions is critical. That's what I love about each of you; you all are my accountability partners and I hope that you know I am here to serve as yours."

As I sat in this circle of elite warriors, I felt like I was back in the huddle with my high school football teammates. The SEALs all had that laser focus and quiet confidence that I used to have when playing quarterback. They also had a bond that can only be built with people who you have invested a lot of time and shared adversity with. I wanted more bonds like that in my life, especially with my wife Erin. She was my best friend and our bond had been weakening over time; at this point, it might have even been broken.

"Hey guys, this might sound like a dumb question, but Coach Kenny said that the only dumb question was the one you don't ask," I said as Coach Kenny smiled and Kyle and Chris both said *Burt Watson* softly under their breath with a laugh. "Do these three building blocks set up the foundation for your family as well?"

"Hooyah, Matthew Simonds," Sean said. "They sure do, and they work in every aspect of life. Once you know the importance of total immersion, spaced repetition and accountability partners, you have the foundation in place for training an elite mindset and training yourself to be successful in anything."

"My wife and I will go on a vacation every 90 days for a total immersion reconnection, and then have a date night once a week as spaced repetition. Then every Sunday we sit down and go over how the last week went: Do we feel like we are living in alignment with our mission, vision and core principles? Are we treating each other with alignment of how we want to live our lives? We are each other's accountability partner and we have a formal accountability meeting every Sunday night where we break this all down.

"This process that I learned from Coach Kenny years ago has been some of the best relationship building she and I have ever done. You have to be super intentional about how you live and how you show up in areas you care about most, like with your family.

Success in combat and in marriage is no different. It happens by intentionally reverse engineering charting a course backwards from your telescope goals to your microscope goals and then following it, while at the same time being able to compensate and adjust on a moment's notice, because life happens. Success is no accident. I can't encourage you guys enough to do the 90-day getaway and be intentional about total immersion, date-night spaced repetition, and weekly accountability check on Sunday night or whatever night works for you. It's been amazing."

Take a vacation every 90 days.

Date night once a week.

Sit-down formal family meeting on Sunday.

I wasn't doing any of that. Erin and I had not been on a vacation, just the two of us, in years and we certainly didn't have a weekly date night.

I needed to be much more intentional about how I was going to show up at home, or I felt like I might not have much of a home to go back to anymore.

CHAPTER 30
AVERAGE OR ELITE MINDSET?

"Matthew Simonds, do you remember when we broke down that list of the differences between an average and an elite mindset?" Coach Kenny asked. "I think this is a good time for us to review that list. Knowing the difference between an average and elite mindset and making the decision to have an elite mindset is a daily commitment and the first step in living *The 10 Pillars of Mental Performance Mastery*."

"Coach Kenny, sorry to cut you off. I think I have the list right here," Sean said as he flipped though Evernote on his phone. "Yes, found it. I'm in the process of typing all our notes from when we worked together, back in college, into my phone using that Evernote app you told me about, and I just did this one several days ago. I'll read it.

"Performers with an average mindset use the phrase *have to*; those with an elite mindset use the phrase *get to* or *want to*.

"Performers with an average mindset focus on how they feel; those with an elite mindset focus on how they act and what they need to do, not how they feel about doing it. Performers with an elite mindset don't let feelings drive them; they let actions drive them.

"Performers with an average mindset make an excuse; those with an elite mindset make it happen.

"Performers with an average mindset feel sorry for themselves. Those with an elite mindset are so focused on others that they don't have time to feel sorry for themselves and know that feeling sorry for themselves is a worthless and useless emotion.

"Performers with an average mindset say it's impossible; those with an elite mindset say it's going to be very difficult.

"Performers with an average mindset see a failure as final, while those with an elite mindset see failure as positive feedback and every setback as a setup for a comeback.

"Performers with an average mindset wear their emotions on their sleeves; those with an elite mindset never show weakness and are always

BIG with their body language so they can be the rock of confidence for others.

"Performers with an average mindset see confidence as a feeling; those with an elite mindset know that confidence is an action.

"Performers with an average mindset focus on what they can't control; those with an elite mindset focus on what they can control."

As Sean read the list, it was very clear to me that I was closer to having an average mindset than I was an elite mindset. And the men I was with unmistakably had an elite mindset.

"Sean, have you always had an elite mindset?" I asked.

"Heck, no!" He laughed. "I always had a fixed mindset and I was an average-mindset performer. A fixed mindset is that you think you can't grow, that you are the way you are. I was stuck in a fixed mindset and getting average results until my freshman year of college when I met Coach Kenny and he invited and challenged me to become more. I can still remember him saying to us as a team, *If you want more, you must become more.* I had always wanted more; I just didn't know how to get there, and Coach Kenny taught us that it all starts with your mindset."

"Hooyah!" the four other SEALs all said in unison.

"Elite mindset is everything and unfortunately most people think that your mindset is fixed, that it is the way it is, and you can't change it or grow it – and that's just not how it is," Sean said. "We saw it all the time in the SEAL Teams. Young men and women come in and are transformed physically, but only after they are transformed mentally. It all starts with the mindset."

"Coach Kenny, you had a simple performance improvement process that you used to teach us. Can you talk about that process?" Sean asked.

"I sure can," Kenny said. "Knowing how performance improvement happens helps you to do it more intentionally and will help you grow an elite mindset as quickly as possible, and we are all trying to do more in less time. Understanding this process is the secret to speeding up the learning curve."

I needed all the speeding up I could get. But I had no idea what the process of performance improvement was that they were talking about.

CHAPTER 31
3 STEPS TO PERFORMANCE IMPROVEMENT

"The three steps to performance improvement or should I say the 3 steps to P.I., will help you speed up the learning curve in all aspects of your life," Coach Kenny said. "The first step (#1) is to increase your awareness, the second (#2) is to have the right strategy and the third step (#3) is to put the strategy into action. These steps to performance improvement are at the foundation of training an elite mindset. You must have awareness, find the right strategy to help you in your given situation, and then put the strategy into action – and the best way to do that is with an accountability partner, support people and a mentor."

Awareness, strategy, action. Total immersion, spaced repetition, accountability partners, support teams and growth plans. That was such a simple and clear process and I had been falling short in all of them. My awareness that my relationship at home was at an all-time low was now at an all-time high. I had never been more aware of how disconnected I was at home. Sean had shared some strategies he used with the 90 day get-a-ways, date night once a week and Sunday sit-downs with his wife; and Coach

Kenny had shared how he sent a text to his wife each morning and either kissed her or FTK'd each night. These were clearly strategies to stay connected and I was going to put them all into action when I got home... if Erin was still around.

"Hey, Sean, when we were at boot camp, how was it that you knew the names of everyone there quicker than anyone else?" Adam asked.

"Yeah, Sean. Are you like a name wizard or born with the name gene?" Kyle asked with a laugh.

"Funny you guys asked," Sean replied. "When I first met Coach Kenny, he blew us all away by walking into the first team meeting and knowing the names of over 100 football players. It was crazy. After that meeting, I couldn't remember anything he said, but I remembered that he knew all of our names. I went right up to him after his talk and asked him how he did it. Coach Kenny, do you remember what you said?"

"I sure do," Coach Kenny answered with a smile and the smirk of a kid on Christmas. "I told you to meet me in my office the next day and I would teach you. That was my way of getting you in there so that I could teach you more about elite mindset and *The 10 Pillars of Mental Performance*

Mastery as it relates to football. You gotta have a hook to get people interested in what you are teaching, and knowing everyone's name before we began was one of my favorite hooks. Also, people don't care what you know until they know that you care, and one of the first signs that you care is that you know someone's name."

"Coach Kenny, of all you have taught me, learning how to memorize names is up near the top of the list," Sean said. *"People don't care what you know till they know that you care, and the first way to show that you care is to know someone's name.* I will always remember when you said that.

"Do you guys want to know how to master names and memorize anything?" Sean asked.

"Hooyah, Sean. If it will help us better connect with people, we want to know – always looking to be a better leader and connect with others and build trust," Kyle said.

I was looking for any way to connect with people. I felt like I had connected with the guys in the room I was in, yet I was not 100% confident I knew them all by name. I knew their names but wasn't confident who was who.

Learning names was going to be a big help to my career. I often forgot people's names as soon as the handshake ended, and I recently lost a big contract because I had called someone by the wrong name.

With names, I needed all the help I could get.

CHAPTER 32
HOW TO REMEMBER ANYTHING

"Men, to memorize anything, you simply need to know three steps; and once you know these three steps you will be amazed at how easily you can memorize names, stories, poems and pretty much anything else," Sean said.

"Is this how you used to share those stories with us as part of your pre-mission motivational briefs?" Chris asked.

"Sure is, Chris," Sean replied. "Let me share with you guys the three steps to memorizing anything, especially names.

"The three steps are (#1) to have a location, (#2) to create a picture, and (#3) to give the picture meaning. That's it."

Location, picture, meaning. I was totally confused.

"Sean, I don't get it. How do a location, picture and meaning help you to memorize people's names?" I asked.

All of a sudden, the six of them started clapping and whistling in a form of celebration. I just put my arms up in the air, still confused.

"Matthew Simonds, we celebrate confusion, questioning and not knowing around here. It's how you grow and we celebrate growth. Remember, no pride, no ego – just progress and learning," Sean said.

"Let me show you. There are seven of us in this room right now. Do you know everyone's name?"

I was on the spot. I knew Coach Kenny and Sean, and I knew that Sean's four SEAL teammates were David, Chris, Kyle and Adam – but I wasn't sure I could tell who was who, and I was embarrassed.

"I think so, but I am not sure, Sean," I replied.

"Matthew Simonds, the first thing people with an elite mindset do when they are around new people they have just met is to learn their names. They are able to do so because they use this strategy," Sean stated. "People with an average mindset are so focused on themselves that they don't take the time to focus on others."

I was definitely focusing more on myself since arriving at Sean's house than I was on getting to know the other guys. Focusing on myself seemed to be a way of life for me and I wanted to change.

"Let me share with you what I do to memorize names," Sean continued. "There are seven of us in this room. Let's make a list that says Location, Picture, Meaning and then I'll show you what I do."

After a few minutes, Sean held up his laptop and showed us all his list.

"Let me explain what I have done here," Sean said. "The first thing to do is find a location on each person that sticks out to you; that's the first thing you see when you look at them.

"The second is to create a picture that you make an association with that has the meaning of their name. For example, any and every Adam I meet I put a picture of the Hoover Dam but instead of there being water behind it, I see ants. Could you imagine that? If you saw that, you would never forget it. So, when I look at Adam and see his beard, I see the Hoover Dam in his beard and ants crawling all over his beard. The ants and the dam mean Adam."

As I looked at each of the men in the room and could put the picture of each that I had written down on their faces, I was able to memorize their names and confidently know who was who.

When I looked at Coach Kenny, I saw a penny and a whistle.

I saw the dam with ants in Adam's beard.

I saw Santa Claus, Kris Kringle, sitting on Chris' head.

I saw the Statue of David atop the nose of David.

I saw a nail file with a *K* surfing on top of the file on top of Kyle's head.

I saw a saw, sawing away on Sean's shaved head.

"Sean, this is amazing. I have never been good at names and I think this will help big time!" I exclaimed.

"It's not that you were never good with names, Matthew Simonds. It's just that you didn't have a strategy. Remember, you are not lacking the ability. You are only blocking your ability, and the way that you unblock your ability is by applying the right strategy. We don't appreciate the importance of strategy. Strategy is everything. Using the right strategy at the right time is the key. and then using strategy in spaced repetition; that's the secret to improvement.

Improve your strategies and the frequency of which you use them," Sean stated. "And as with anything, Matthew Simonds, it's not that you have a good memory or a bad memory; you are simply trained or untrained. Now you are trained in names and how to memorize and you can be trained in anything."

"Matthew Simonds, like any new skill you learn, you will go through a progression of acceptance or a progression of buy-in. You will also go through a progression of commitment," Coach Kenny said. "These are very much like the stages your clients, or should I say friends, go through when you work with them as a consultant. Do you know the stages of acceptance/buy-in and commitment?"

"No sir, I don't," I replied.

But boy, was I excited to learn.

CHAPTER 33
GETTING ACCEPTANCE/BUY-IN

"Matthew Simonds, anytime you, or anyone, for that matter, are learning something new, you go through a four-stage process that we in the MPM Coaching world refer to as the four stages of acceptance/buy-in. Those four stages are (#1) this ain't for me, (#2) this might be OK for others, (#3) I'll try it, (#4) I can't believe I did it any other way. We all go through these four stages, and once you know this about humans and our psychology, you can more easily evaluate where you're at or where the people you're working with are at in buying into what you are teaching."

This made total sense to me. When Sean started talking about going on a vacation with his wife every 90 days and doing a date night once a week, I first met his idea with some resistance and said to myself, *I can't do that; I have too much work to do; that might be OK for him to do, but I can't do that.* I went through stages 1-2 right there.

Then as he started talking more, I think I got to stage 3 where I said, *I'll try it.* It's my hope that when I get home and start taking Erin on a date night once a week that I will look back and say, *I can't believe I did it any other way.*

"I went through those four stages with almost everything in boot camp," Kyle chuckled.

I knew it was Kyle because I saw the nail file with a surfing K on top of his head as I looked at him. Come to think of it, I just went through the four stages of acceptance/buy-in with the name memorization strategy of location, picture and meaning.

I tried it, it worked for me, and I couldn't believe that I had made it this far in life without having a specific name memorization strategy.

"Now that we have covered the four stages of acceptance/buy-in, let's cover the four stages of commitment," Coach Kenny said. "But first, I need to get some more black coffee so I can commit to being razor sharp with my focus and energy this morning. At my age, caffeine is as at times as necessary as oxygen."

We all laughed and walked over to the kitchen to refuel with black coffee. It was a much-needed break, since my hand was getting sore from all of the notes I was taking.

CHAPTER 34
CREATING COMMITMENT

When we got back from the kitchen, we sat down in our seats and all reached for our notebooks.

"Does anyone remember the four stages of commitment?" Sean asked.

"I think I got them, boss," David said. "(#1) Do a job, (#2) do work, (#3) have a career, (#4) go on a mission. Is that right?"

"Hooyah, David!" Sean answered him with a smile.

"Matthew Simonds, we all go through these four stages of commitment and we go from stage to stage on a weekly and sometimes daily or hourly basis," Coach Kenny said. "The key is to always be focused on your mission. To keep reconnecting to your why and to your mission.

"When we get started in a career or in a relationship, our focus is razor sharp, our energy is positive, our awareness is heightened. We do everything with intention. We are on a mission. Then over time we slide into a rut and focus on what we do as a career because we lose connection with the meaning of why we do what we do. We can even slip out of having a career to doing work or, at the worst, what we do becomes a job. When we lose focus of why we do what we do, we fall off the mission and into a career, work or job. We are always best when we keep a one-day-contract mentality and day-one energy."

"Well said, Coach Kenny." Sean reiterated: "When you are mission focused, you really have a big reason why and know exactly what you are after and why you are after it. This elevated focus helps you to minimize the distractions that are around us 24/7 and helps you to say *no* to the smaller issues and traps that will take you away from the bigger mission. We have to always remember that the main thing is to keep the main thing the main thing."

As I sat there taking notes, I realized that I was far from being on a mission. I was stuck in a job. What I did as a business consultant was at one point a mission for me, a mission to make a positive impact in the lives of others. I could trace my drifting from the mission into a career, work and now a job back to when my mindset shifted from influence and impact to income because I had lost the bigger reason why. It had become about me and not about those I was there to serve. I was walking into a room and saying, "Here I am" vs. walking in and saying "There you are." My whole life had become about me, and it was sickening.

"Sean, I think I have fallen off my mission and landed in the land of the Job. What do you think I should do?" I asked.

As Sean sat back and took a deep breath, I looked around the room and it seemed like everyone was staring at me.

CHAPTER 35
ASK MORE ELITE QUESTIONS

"Matthew Simonds, let's continue here with building an elite mindset. You need to ask yourself more elite questions. Those who ask more elite questions climb to a more elite status. The best coaches are the best question askers. We have to start by asking elite questions and know that we all fall off the mission more than we would like to; you're not alone," Sean responded as the other men all chimed in with "Hooyah, Matthew Simonds."

"Asking yourself elite questions will help you regain your best focus and help you get back on your mission," Sean said. "Here are some of my favorite elite questions:

1. If you had three days left to live, and one of them had to be invested into service to others, what would you do?
2. If you had all the money and all the time in the world, what would you do?
3. Fast forward to your funeral, graduation or retirement and imagine your children, wife, family, friends and those who you worked with being there and speaking about you.

> What would you want them to say about you at that event?

"These are just some of my favorite elite questions. When you answer these questions, you will get more clarity on your mission. Men, I answer questions every year on December 31; why don't we all do it together right now?" Sean asked.

As we all started writing, I felt a little lost. I was confused. In the past, I would beat myself up and call myself an idiot for not knowing or for being confused. Today I celebrated that feeling.

I was excited to refocus myself on my two most important missions, my family and my consulting career... now my consulting *mission* where I was blessed to educate, empower and energize others to be their best. I wasn't doing great at living my mission right now, but I wanted to get back to it.

After writing for about five minutes in silence, Sean got up to answer the phone.

When he walked back in, he said, "Men, do you remember Jason, the former SEAL Team operator I played football with in college?"

"Sure do," said Kyle. "That guy was a beast."

"Well, he just called and is in town," Sean stated. "He is going to the Dominators vs. Beez game today and asked if we all wanted to go. He has eight extra tickets. His position coach in college is the current Dominators head coach, Tony Shay. He said we could meet with Coach Shay before the game if we could get over there early enough. You guys want to go?"

"I'm in," Kyle answered.

"In," David said.

"All in for that," Chris replied.

"Roger that. I'm in," Adam said.

"I would love that. I'm in," Coach Kenny said.

Then they all looked at me. Erin and the kids were home in Arizona. I was going to either try and get a rental car and drive there or try to find a flight. This, however, was a once-in-a-lifetime experience and one I wanted to take part in. I had never been to a PFL football game on Thanksgiving, had never met a PFL football coach, and Tony Shay was the hottest coach in the game. I was also truly enjoying my time with my new friends.

As of now, there were no rental cars available and no flights to Arizona till Saturday. I didn't know what to do.

"In," I said as I went with my gut to keep learning from these guys so that I could be better in the long run.

"Hooyah!" they all cheered.

"OK, I will let Jason know that we're in. We have more to cover here about training an elite mindset and I want to finish learning about all of your elite mindsets, so we are going to have to pick up the pace," Sean said. "Talking about an elite mindset and education is much more important than the entertainment value of going to a football game. We can do both – we will just have to boogie a bit.

"I am jacked up to meet with Coach Shay. I have only read great things about him and his ability as a leader and how he has transformed the culture of the Dominators. Why don't we do this? Let's (#1) finish our talk here on elite mindset, then (#2) hit a shower and (#3) head to the game."

"Hooyah," I said as all of them looked at me and laughed.

"OK, I'll call Jason and let him know we will be heading over there and then we will continue crush learning about elite mindset. Let's roll!" Sean exclaimed.

CHAPTER 36
MAKE YOUR BED

As Sean was on the phone with Jason, he walked into the room I had slept in, walked out with a smile on his face and sat back down as he hung up the phone.

"OK, men. We are all set," he said. "Matthew Simonds, do you know why I just walked into your room?"

"No sir," I replied.

"I wanted to check to see if you were making your bed every morning first thing when you wake up. You remember, this is one of the first things they teach you at SEAL training."

"With all due respect, Sean, is making your bed really a key to building an elite mindset?" I asked.

"Sure is!" Sean exclaimed. "When you make your bed, you start a domino effect of habits that trigger an elite mindset, self-control, discipline and habits of excellence. I'll share with you why I make my bed:

1. You are immediately acting differently than how you feel because nobody feels like making their bed, and acting differently than how you feel is an essential component of an elite mindset.

2. You are paying attention to detail. Paying attention to detail is a critical part of an elite mindset – the details of your relationship, the details of the mission, the details of your physical and financial futures, the details of simply making your bed. Part of why we make our bed is to reinforce the attention to detail that it takes to be the best you that you can be.

3. Making your bed also shows that you have self-discipline over yourself, which is critical in anything you do. Without discipline to put off what you want in the moment for what you want most, you will get sucked up by the temptations around you.

4. You also start your day with a win, and if your day is total chaos, which it can often be, at least you come home to an already-made bed – and that is a sign that tomorrow will be a better day.

5. You also start your day in a routine and reinforcing that you are committed to habits of excellence. The more aspects of

our life that we can turn over to routine and habits, the more consistent we will be and the more energy we will have for bigger-picture ideas, rather than getting fatigued from deciding if we are going to make our bed or deciding what we are going to eat or wear.

"As SEALs, we were trained to be machines of routine so that we could operate in chaotic environments without having to think; we could just react, sink to our training and respond. This commitment to routine is also reinforced through making your bed."

I had no idea that there were so many benefits to making your bed. When I stopped and thought about it, they made sense to me. I also thought that Sean's reasons for making your bed all reinforced mindsets and aspects of *The 10 Pillars of Mental Performance Mastery* that would serve me well in life.

"You know, guys," Kyle said, "every morning in boot camp, my instructors would show up in my room and the first thing they would inspect was my bed. They were checking to see if I did it right – if the corners were square, if the covers were pulled tight, if the pillow was centered just under the headboard and if the extra blanket was folded neatly at the foot of the bed.

"It was a simple task and every morning we were required to make our beds to perfection. It didn't make sense to me at the time; we were training to be SEALs, not maids, but the genius of this simple act has been proven to me many times over and reinforces exactly what Sean is talking about with why he does it."

"It really does," David agreed. "When you make your bed every morning, you accomplish the first task of the day and that will give you the momentum to do another task, and then the ball keeps rolling from there. Once you get Uncle Mo [momentum] on your side, you just keep rolling and one task becomes two, becomes three, becomes four; and next thing you know, you have put together one heck of a productive day. Always remember, present, process, productive, the 3P's."

"It also reinforces that there are only two ways to do anything – the right way and again. If you can't do the little things right, you will never have the time or be able to do the big things right," Coach Kenny said.

It made so much sense – a simple routine to start your day that I had been taking for granted my whole life.

"I've never been more fired up to make my bed before than I am right now," I said with a laugh.

"The key is consistency, Matthew Simonds," Sean responded. "Anyone can get fired up and be a "Go Hard" as my friend, MPM certified coach and former Major League Baseball Player Eric Byrnes likes to call them, for a short period of time – just listen to the hottest motivational speaker on YouTube – but that's short-term. Those with an elite mindset are trained to be able to stay focused, motivated and inside of their routine when things are not going well and when the bullets are flying. This is a learned skill that takes time to develop. There are no shortcuts on the highway to excellence and an elite mindset. You must do the work and put in the time. You must be a Go Hard all the time, not just when you feel like it."

"Hooyah, Sean," Adam said. "Staying in my routine when the bullets were flying saved my life a few times."

"There is a reason why most people fall out of their routine and get into a RUT-TINE," Sean stated. "Let's talk about something which is easy to say and hard to do, but it's an essential part of the elite mindset-building process."

CHAPTER 37
NEVER FEEL SORRY FOR YOURSELF

"When adversity hits, most people will start to feel sorry for themselves, and feeling sorry for yourself is a worthless and useless emotion that will only hold you back from progress," Sean said. "People who have an elite mindset NEVER feel sorry for themselves; they are too busy thinking about the solution rather than focusing on the problems from the past."

I laughed. I spent most of my time on the road feeling sorry for myself that I wasn't home and most of my time at home feeling sorry for myself that I wasn't on the road making money. I had fallen deep into one of the RUT-TINES that Sean was talking about.

"Adversity is necessary in the pursuit of success. Failure and success are neighbors on the highway to excellence. Adversity is to be celebrated and embraced, not avoided," Sean continued. "If we avoid adversity, then we feel sorry for ourselves when we don't get the result we are looking for. People with an elite mindset get fascinated, not frustrated; they get encouraged, not discouraged; and they seek adversity because they know that inside of every adversity is a learning opportunity and that the world belongs to the learner."

"Winners and learners," I said.

"Hooyah, Matthew Simonds," Kyle shouted.

"A key mindset shift that I made when I was training for the Olympics was to trade expectation for appreciation," Coach Kenny said. "That mindset shift helped me to move from feeling sorry for myself when I didn't get my result or if I didn't like what we were doing that day. It also allowed me to be more appreciative of what we were doing and allowed me to live with more of an attitude of gratitude. When you have more gratitude in your life, you feel less sorry for yourself and complain less. Nobody likes being around people who complain all the time."

"You know, Coach Kenny, I remember you talking about an Attitude of Gratitude journal when you spoke to our team all those years ago," Sean said. "I started keeping an Attitude of Gratitude journal and writing down five things I was grateful for on a daily basis. I shared this with all of the men I worked with in the SEAL teams, and I think I heard more positive feedback on this than maybe anything else."

"I still do it," Kyle stated.

"Roger that. Did mine this morning on my phone before we ran," Adam said.

I thought that making your bed was an easy add to my morning routine; this was another one that I thought I could include in my morning routine and would help set me up for success the rest of the day. I knew I could use more positivity in my life.

"The challenge with making your bed and keeping an Attitude of Gratitude journal is the law of the two easies. The two easies, so easy to do, it's also easy not to do." Coach Kenny said. "We call that the law of two easies. So easy to do, it's also easy not to do. I thought that was worth repeating. Why don't we all write down five things we are grateful for and make the commitment the rest of this day to not feel sorry for ourselves but to enjoy the time we have together, to trade expectation for appreciation, and to DOMINATE this day at the highest level."

"Hooyah, Coach Kenny," Sean exclaimed. "DOMINATE the Day!"

As I wrote down the five things I was grateful for, I knew I would benefit from not feeling sorry for myself that I wasn't with Erin and the kids. I'd get more out of being into what we were doing here than just being in the room.

MY FIVE: ATTITUDE OF GRATITUDE
1. Erin and her amazing energy
2. Brina and Michael and their innocence
3. Yotie and Cypress and how cute they are
4. Coach Kenny for teaching me the 10 Pillars of MPM
5. Sean for teaching me more details and strategies for building elite mindset

"Once you guys write down your five, I want you to stand up and we'll share," Sean said.

As we stood up to share, I felt a nervous excitement. I didn't know these guys all that much but felt closer to them than I did to most people I knew. Just being in their presence was empowering.

As we shared our Attitude of Gratitude journals, I felt the bond between us all getting stronger.

CHAPTER 38
FLIP THE SWITCH & NEVER SHOW WEAKNESS

"Thank you for sharing, guys. When you share your gratitude and give it away, you get more gratitude coming your way," Coach Kenny said. "I now want you to look around the room. Look at the body language of each other. How each other is standing. Now I want you all to just pull your shoulders back and straighten up your spine. I want you to GET BIG with your body language and straight with your spine because a straight spine is an alert mind."

As I pulled my shoulders back and stood tall, I realized that I had not stood this tall since I was a high school football player. Coach Allen used to make us always stand tall, especially after sprints. When we were all gasping for air, he would coach us to stand tall and never show weakness, to say out loud that we wanted more, that we would never quit and we had more in us.

"Men, stay in this big state with big body language. Never show weakness," Coach Kenny stated. "Never showing weakness is always being big and confident with your body language when you flip that switch on to compete. Be big because your physiology affects your psychology – and vice versa, your psychology affects your physiology. We are often more aware of our bodies than of our minds, so consciously making the effort to GET BIG and to never show weakness will help you unlock your elite mindset and perform at a higher level. In the heat of battle and business, there isn't time to feel sorry for yourself; you just need to stay big and move forward.

"Never showing weakness is about being big and confident. It's also about being real and vulnerable. Don't be confused. Crying and embracing those you love and being real when the switch is off and you are not in competition mode is a sign of strength and that you are comfortable in your own skin. Getting frustrated and complaining, playing small – that is showing weakness. Think about it like this: When you flip the competition switch on, never show weakness; when you have the switch off, you can show emotions and weakness. You are not a robot. You are a performer and a person. Know who you need to be in that moment, and when you flip the switch on, act as if it were impossible to fail."

"That makes sense, Coach Kenny. I cry all the time, man. I love you guys and never tell you that enough. You guys are family, you are my brothers. Know that I would do anything for any of you at any time," Sean said as his eyes welled up and his voice started to crack. "When I was younger, I thought that expressing positive emotion was a sign of weakness; now I realize that it's a sign of strength. When we are in combat and competition, we need to keep that front-sight focus on the mission; but when the mission is over, we need to be real and tap into the emotional side of life. Learning to flip the switch on and off is critical. When the switch is on we are unbreakable, when it is off we are vulnerable."

Sean walked around and gave each person in the circle a hug. When he came up to me, he put his hands on my shoulders and looked me in the eye through the tears in his eyes.

"Matthew Simonds, you are welcome in this house anytime," Sean said. "I speak for all of us when I say that we are here to help you with anything you need, and it sounds like you are going through some tough times at home and in your life. We are here as your teammates, as your brothers and as your accountability partners to help you on your mission."

A tear ran down my cheek as I thanked Sean with a 20 second hug. I thanked Kyle, Chris, Adam and David. Then when I got to Coach Kenny, I lost it. He had done so much for me in such a short period of time and had made more impact on my life in less than 24 hours than anyone had since Coach Allen in high school, and I was with him for four years.

"Matthew Simonds. This is life and we only get one chance at playing this game I'm not sure anyone can ever get this game right," Coach Kenny said. "No pride, no ego, just progress and learning. We are here for you."

CHAPTER 39
STAY PATIENT IN THE FACE OF ADVERSITY

"You must learn to stay patient in the face of adversity. To know that if you are still alive you are too blessed to be stressed," Coach Kenny explained. "Getting worked up and stressed out does nothing to help you perform in this moment because in this moment that's all there is – this moment. When we start to press and get all into red lights, it's because we are focused on the past or the future. Remember, depression is obsession with the past and anxiety is obsession with the future, optimal performance is obsession with the present."

"And I am going to the bathroom all over the present," I said, laughing as Coach Kenny lowered his hands from my shoulders.

"Exactly!" Coach Kenny exclaimed. "Staying patient in the face of adversity is about being able to be where your feet are and live in this moment. Present, process, productive."

I remembered Coach Allen always telling us to compete one play at a time, to breathe pre-snap as part of our routine so that we could break up the game play by play and be more in control of our emotions. He used to say that emotion clouds reality and that oxygen clarifies reality. That the one-play warrior lives and fights for this play only and then repeats that process for as many plays as it takes.

"Staying patient in the face of adversity is critical in combat. When the bullets start flying, you are finished if you lose your head," Sean said. "You have to stay in control of yourself before you can be in control of your performance. Staying in control of yourself is easier said than done, but like anything else related to mindset and mental toughness, it's a trainable skillset."

"How do you train your ability to stay patient in the face of adversity?" I asked. "I could sure use that with my wife, kids and the French Bulldogs at home. Your dogs haven't moved off their beds; mine won't go near theirs."

"We can all use more patience, Matthew Simonds," Sean replied. "Remember, when you get stressed, you start to press and what you need to do is breathe. In boot camp we used to do a meditation practice that we called the 6-2-8 breath on a daily basis. You would simply inhale for 6, hold for 2 and then exhale for 8.

"We would start by doing this training in a quiet and controlled environment and then move into an environment where we were doing this under extreme stress. We found that by training our breath, we were able to stay in control of ourselves in extreme stress situations because we had conditioned ourselves to do so. One of the key principles of SEAL training is relentless fundamental execution under extreme stress. Let's practice, shall we?"

Sean instructed us all to sit up straight in our chairs with our feet flat on the floor and with our hands in our laps. As we inhaled for 6, held for 2 and exhaled for 8, we were to then open up one finger from our slightly closed hands and repeat this till we were able to do 10 breaths without breaking focus.

As we started the exercise, I made it about halfway through the second breath when my mind started racing to how I was going to get home, mend my relationships with Erin, Brina and Michael, and how I was going to stop working so much so that I could get home.

As I squinted my eyes to look around the room at the other guys, I noticed that they were all locked in, one breath at a time. They were in a meditative state like we experienced at the end of the yoga session earlier this morning.

"Sean, I made it through about two breaths before I got distracted. Is that normal?" I asked when they were all done.

"It sure is, Matthew," Sean said. "Learning to stay patient in adversity is part of a mindset and you build that skill through meditation, which is part of pillar #6. Patience in adversity is only achieved after learning to stay patient when there is no adversity. Staying patient is a practice that you must train like any skill or anything that you have learned today about training an elite mindset. Just like we did yoga this morning, the 6-2-8 exercise should become part of your daily Mental Performance Mastery training routine. You will notice that your ability to stay patient in the face of adversity will strengthen just like a muscle as you increase your commitment to training."

I was committed to becoming more patient, whether through yoga practice or the 6-2-8 breathing exercise. I wanted to be able to stay more patient in the face of adversity. Erin was much better at this than I was and now I realized it was largely due to her yoga practice. Yet another reason for me to start going to her classes.

CHAPTER 40
YOU DON'T RISE TO THE OCCASION; YOU SINK TO YOUR TRAINING AND HABITS

"My first time through boot camp we had an instructor that said something similar, he said that you must be able to keep your head when all others around you are losing theirs. He said that you would not rise up to a challenge, but sink to your training.

This philosophy is the foundation of *You don't rise to the occasion; you sink to your levels of training and habits,*" Sean said. "You become what you do on a daily basis. You don't rise to the occasion; you sink to your levels of training and habits."

These were mindsets that Coach Allen had taught to us when I was in high school. How could I have forgotten them? They were so simple yet so powerful and had helped me so much as a football player.

"Sean, I think I have heard this before," I said.

"You probably have, Matthew Simonds," Sean replied. "Time-tested principles will be around forever if they work. This one works; the question is, are you working it? All of these 10 pillars of mental performance mastery will work when you work them."

"I'm not sure what you mean, Sean," I said.

"Look, you don't sink to the levels of your knowledge and you don't sink to what you know. You sink to what you train, to what you practice on a daily basis under stress," Sean responded. "K-A=0. You men remember that one?"

"Sure do," Kyle quipped. "Knowledge minus Action gets you Nothing. The man who does will beat the man who knows all day long."

"Matthew Simonds, the key is to make your habits so strong and your training so good that when you sink to your worst day, you sink to a level higher than anyone else on their best day," Coach Kenny said. "It's easy to say, hard to do, and only possible if you follow the 10 pillars of mental performance mastery."

The only habits I had currently were sleeping in till the last minute, finding excuses for not exercising and finding more reasons to work than to invest into my family. I knew I needed to change. I just didn't really know how.

"How do you change bad habits?" I asked the group.

"The first step is to remember that your eyes are on the front of your head and that you have to look forward more than you look backwards," Sean answered. "The past is a platform for learning, while the future is a fortress of unlimited possibilities. It's a lot like driving a car. You have the windshield and the rearview mirror. You have the rearview mirror to look at where you have been and to see if anything is creeping up on you. You spend 80-90% of the time looking in the windshield and you want to do the same thing here. Look briefly at your past self, acknowledge that you are not where you want to be, and then bring your focus back to where you are driving right now, to this moment. Then see the habits you must create and what you must do each day to build yourself and your mindset so strong that when you sink, you sink to a level of excellence."

"Is this a part of why we make our bed in the morning?" I asked.
"Exactly!" Sean replied. "Everyone talks about raising the roof. In reality, it's about raising your basement so that you have good bad days and

are better on your bad days than most people are on their good days – because you can focus better and have better habits and a more elite mindset. It's really about being the best version of you that you have ever been. It's also about not comparing yourself to anyone else but comparing yourself today to where you were yesterday. If you can see progress – be better today than you were yesterday and better tomorrow than you are today – and just keep going baby step by baby step, you will get to where you want to be."

"Hooyah, Sean!" Adam responded. "Raise the basement."

"But know this, Matthew Simonds," Sean said as he squinted his eyes and intensified his focus. "In the pursuit of becoming the best you that you can be, life doesn't become easier. It actually becomes harder. The group of average – you know, the best of the worst and the worst of the best – they will try to suck you in, and the higher you elevate your mindset, the greater the pull from the land of average will be to bring you back to their level."

 "It's like crabs when I used to go crabbing in Maryland," David commented. "When you caught one crab, you had to put a lid on the bucket or it would climb up the side and escape. As soon as you caught two or more, you could take the lid off because the crabs would not let each other climb to that next level and escape. It's a big part of why it's so important to know that you become the average of the five people you hang out with most – luckily for us, we spent a lot of time together and helped each other grow into the men we are today. Not everyone has that luxury to be around people who are elite, but everyone can read about people who are elite and spend more time reading and listening to those who are elite through things like podcasts and books than swimming with the sea of average."

1. Raise your basement.
2. Look through the windshield.
3. Don't let the crabs pull you down.
4. You become the average of the five people you hang out with most and the five things you do daily.

I couldn't write fast enough and these guys weren't slowing down anytime soon. They were masters of elite mindset. Ironically, I had heard Coach Allen say much of what they were saying back in high school.

CHAPTER 41
THE ONLY EASY DAY WAS YESTERDAY

"Men, remember that the only easy day was yesterday," David said. "That when you are in the pursuit of becoming more, of becoming your best, life becomes harder. Don't get me wrong. It becomes immensely more enjoyable, but it also becomes harder. As you grow, you will see the world differently and you will focus more on others than you do yourself. They will create more demands on you and your time, and with that, more opportunities to give back and make a difference will arise. You can do anything, but you can't do everything. It's a balancing act for sure. There is good and bad to everything."

"*The only easy day was yesterday* reminds me of something that you hear coaches talk about who have won World or NCAA National Championships. They say that once you win, the expectation becomes that you win it every year," Sean said. "And we know that pressure causes some people to break but causes others to break records and to break through.

"The key to living with an elite mindset is knowing that you are going to have to get up and prove yourself to yourself every day. When you can hold yourself to this standard, then in fact the only easy day becomes yesterday, not because of what others are demanding of you, but because you hold yourself to such a high standard that to not perform better or be more present than you were the day before shows a sign of complacency – and complacency kills. You must stay hungry and you must keep growing, not because you have to but because you want to; and when you keep growing, life keeps getting better and harder, which is GOOD.

"The only easy day was yesterday because you are on a mission to give more today than you did yesterday. This focus, in my opinion, is the secret to optimal living – being more so you can give more of yourself to others to help them become more. It's a great cycle."

As I sat there listening to David, Sean and the others talk about the only easy day being yesterday, I started to think about how difficult my day had been yesterday, the difficult conversations I'd had with Erin, and that it looked like I was going to miss Thanksgiving and her birthday. I sure hoped that today and tomorrow were going to be more positive and easier than yesterday because that was a tough one.

"Matthew Simonds," Coach Kenny called. "Remember in life there are winners and ....?"

"Learners!" I shouted.

"While the world belongs to the learner, we live in a bottom-line world," Coach Kenny said. "You have to produce in your job, in your mission, or you will get fired. The Detroit Dominators must win or their coaches will get fired. You must be present in your relationship or you will get divorced. The bottom line is that when you talk outcome, there are winners and *losers*; you just can't look at it like that. You have to intentionally choose the winners and *learners* mindset. This is a competitive world we live in, and the world belongs to the learner.

"Again, it's a balance. You want to win and you want to learn. You must want to learn more than you want to win to become the performer you want to be. Michael Jordan did this. Georges St. Pierre did this. The best of the best in any field have this mentality. They want to win; they want to win badly and often at all costs. They just want to learn more because they know that learning is what helps them to keep winning."

I was loving the *winners and learners* philosophy. It made sense to me. You had to produce to get results (win) and the world is competitive (winners and losers). Yet, life is a triathlon; it's a long race to be your best and you need multiple skill sets to succeed. The biggest winners are the learners, and the learners win more than anyone else.

CHAPTER 42
IT PAYS TO BE A WINNER

"It pays... WHAT?" Coach Kenny shouted at the group.

"It pays to be a winner!" they all shouted.

"Matthew Simonds. You are a winner, my friend," Coach Kenny stated. "When you were born, you outswam over one million sperm to even step foot into this world."

"That's a good point, Coach," I said with a laugh.

"Some people will tell you that winning isn't all that important. That's probably because they don't ever win," Coach Kenny said. "I will tell you that all these years later it still bothers me that I didn't win a medal in the Olympics. But I don't let that weigh me down; I use it as fuel to push me further.

"Winners get more opportunities in life. They get more attention. They get more fame and they get more fortune," Coach Kenny continued. "The key is to always keep a learner's perspective ahead of a winner's perspective or you won't keep winning. It's also key to know that to WIN is to focus on What's Important Now.

"Here is what I want you all to do. We are going to make a short list of what I call the three most important things you must do right now to help you get closer to being the best version of you that you can be. That's the ultimate win, to be the best version of you that you can be and to live life as the highest and best version of you, in a constant and never-ending growth state."

As we all wrote down our three, I knew I wanted to be the best version of myself. I wanted to keep growing; I wanted to live life at the highest level. I wanted to have more of an elite mindset like Sean and Coach Kenny. I just wasn't sure where to start.

"Coach Kenny, I am struggling. Where do I get started?" I asked.

All of the men clapped in a celebration of my struggle. They celebrated that I was confused and working through the process to understand how to become more.

"Matthew Simonds, it's the start that stops most people. You don't have to get it right to get started, but you must get started to get it right," Coach Kenny said. "You just wrote down the first three important things that came to mind that you need to do now to be the best you that you can be. You can always compensate and adjust as you grow. What did you write?"

I wrote the following:

1. Make my bed and get up in the 5am Club.
2. Have a routine date night with Erin each week.
3. Do yoga at least once a week with Erin and start doing the 6-2-8 breathing exercise once a day.

"You could probably have written out more, but once you get to three, you must stop!" Coach Kenny said. "Remember, you can do anything, but you can't do everything. If you have more than three goals, you don't have ANY!"

You can do anything; you can't do everything.

If you have more than three goals, you don't have any.

I felt like we were back in Protector Brewery and Burger and I was drinking from the fire hydrant of knowledge that was Coach Kenny and *The 10 Pillars of Mental Performance Mastery*. Everything that Sean, Coach Kenny and the SEALs said was pure gold and challenged my current average mindset, and I loved it.

Internally I was celebrating that challenge to my mindset. I knew that to have more and give more I needed to become more.

"Hey, we gotta finish up so that we can get to the game and go see Jason and meet with Coach Shay," Sean said. "Let's finish up, recap, hit the shower and then hit the road. We are going to need to get some food as well – I am starving!"

"Roger that!" Adam agreed.

I hadn't noticed how hungry I was because I was eating up so much of this elite mindset training. I did notice that my right hand was sore from all the note taking, but it was a pain I gladly welcomed. After all, Coach Allen used to tell us all the time that pain was just weakness leaving the body.

CHAPTER 43
THE RACE TO EXCELLENCE
HAS NO FINISH LINE

After we all shared our list of three, I realized how similar what I shared was to what the others had shared. I realized that I wasn't alone in my desire to become more, invest more into my marriage, and to get up out of bed in the morning before 6am so that I could be a member of the 5am Club and start dominating the day.

As different as I thought these guys would be, we were more alike than I had thought.

They had more awareness, better strategy, took more action, had a more elite mindset and stronger set of accountability partners than I had.

They were much more elite in their mindset than I was, but I could clearly see that if I started to live with more purpose and intention I could become more elite by building an elite mindset and living *The 10 Pillars of Mental Performance Mastery*.

"Men, there is one more concept related to elite mindset that I want to go over. It's the understanding that when you are in pursuit of excellence, of being the best and highest version of you that you are capable of, there is no finish line. It's a race you run and there is no finish line. You are never done. You never reach the tape in this race," Sean stated. "You never become excellent or elite; you are always in pursuit of excellence and becoming elite. Once you think you have arrived, you stop learning, your pride and ego get in the way and start increasing your chances of losing; and as a SEAL, that often- meant death. So we took the concept of excellence – no pride, no ego, just progress and learning and the commitment to always working to be the best version of you – very seriously."

Excellence is a race with no finish line. I liked that.

"Matthew Simonds, the key is to always be in a growth mindset. To never settle, to never become complacent because, as you already learned, complacency kills," Coach Kenny said. "You want to have a humble confidence – the humility to know that you must train and keep growing or you will get passed by, and the confidence to know that when it's time to go hard and time to perform you are ready and prepared to flip the switch and execute at the highest level. You want to have the confidence that you have prepared and that your separation from your previous self and the competition is in your preparation. Prepare, perform, recover, repeat. It's a simple process, yet we as humans make everything more complex than it needs to be."

Prepare, perform, recover, repeat. I loved it!

As we all chuckled and nodded in agreement with that, Sean stood up.

"All right, men," he said. "Let's wrap it up and move out. Know that excellence has no finish line and that working on yourself is a neverending process and race that we will gladly run as long as we are able. As long as we can put one foot in front of the other, we will run our race and give our best. We will eventually cross the finish line of our life and be glad we ran as hard as we could till the very end."

"Hooyah, Sean," we all said together.

"Again, I can't thank you enough, Sean, for letting me stay here last night," I said. "Thank you, Coach Kenny, for teaching me *The 10 Pillars of*

Mental Performance Mastery and to all of you guys for sharing with me what you know about building an elite mindset. I have heard a lot of this stuff we talked about today regarding mindset before; I just haven't always lived it. Today was a great refresher. As you guys have said, you are either growing or you are dying, you never stay the same. Today I grew."

"In our weight room at the SEAL base in Baghdad we had a sign that said, *The enemy thanks you for taking a day off and taking shortcuts."* Sean said. "Day by day we get better in every way."

"Hooyah, men!" Coach Kenny said.

"Can we review to make sure that I got them all? I don't want to miss anything," I asked.

"Let's roll, Matthew Simonds," Sean said. "Fire away 'cause we got to get to that game."

CHAPTER 44
ELITE MINDSET REVIEW

As I read my notes about elite mindset, I saw the others nod along with me, which gave me confidence that I had gotten them right. I read:

1. Awareness, strategy action.
2. Total immersion, spaced repetition and growth plans with accountability partners.
3. Location, picture meaning.
4. Not for me, OK for others, I'll try it, I can't believe I did it any other way.
5. Job, work, career, mission.
6. Make your bed.
7. Never feel sorry for yourself.
8. Never show weakness.
9. Stay patient in the face of adversity.
10. You don't rise to the occasion; you sink to your levels of training and habits.
11. The only easy day was yesterday.
12. It pays to be a winner.
13. Excellence has no finish line.

"Hooyah, Matthew Simonds," Sean said. "That's a good list. You will get more, I am sure, when you listen to this recording, but you basically nailed it. Now pick one to three and get to work. We good here, men?"

After everyone gave confirmation that they were good, I reached down to turn off my phone, which had been audio recording the entire session. As I picked up my phone and turned off the voice memos app, I realized I had missed a call from Erin.

"All right, men. Let's hit the showers and then head over to see Jason, Coach Shay, and the Dominators and Beez, oh my," Sean said with a laugh at his Wizard of Oz reference. "Let's roll out on the hour, which is in 15 minutes."

"Roger that, Sean," everyone confirmed.

As I walked back to my room, I called Erin and there was no answer. Rather than leaving a message, I sent her a text that said: *Good morning, my love. Happy Thanksgiving. Working to find a way home. Give me a call when you are free.*

I was excited to talk to Erin and the kids. I was also excited to go to the game with these guys and to meet Jason and Coach Shay.

CHAPTER 45
THE PHONE CALL

After I made my bed, I jumped in the shower and went ice cold as long as I could. After the 30-second shower, I got out and changed clothes as fast as I could.

I wasn't going to be the one responsible for slowing this team of high train alpha males down.

As I neatly hung my towel to dry, I noticed I had missed a callback from Erin while I was in the shower.

She had sent me a text to call her ASAP.

As I was walking out of the room to join the other guys downstairs, I called and she answered.

"Hey, Baby," I said. "Happy Thanksgiving."

After a few more seconds than normal and a few more seconds than I had anticipated, she spoke.

"Matthew," she said, fighting back tears. "We have a problem."

CHAPTER 46
DECISION TIME

As I hung up the phone, I could feel a pit in my stomach. I was torn. Should I just go back to the airport and see if I can get on any flights back home or should I call all of the rental car agencies again? I had a decision to make.

I knew that I should be with Erin, Michael and Brina during this time of year. I also wanted to keep learning from Coach Kenny and the SEALs.

Then I remembered a key principle that Coach Allen had taught us in high school: There are times in life when what you want to do and what you should do are not going to match up. Times when you have to put off what you want to do in the moment for what you want most. TImes when delayed gratification becomes critical. He used to say that it was in those moments that our lives were truly shaped. That one conversation, one book, one decision could truly change your life forever.

I wanted to be with my family but I felt as if I should stay where I was so that I could continue to grow for my family. It felt a bit selfish but I truly was becoming more by being around these men. I knew that if I were going to save my marriage, be the ultimate father I could be and get myself going in the right direction, I needed to keep drinking from the fire hose that had been the last few hours with the guys. Not only was I having fun, I was learning a ton. When you can have fun and learn a ton, you know you are in the right place.

It was decision time. I was going to go to the game, keep learning, and keep trying to call the airlines and rental car companies to see if I could get out any earlier.

CHAPTER 47
BODY LANGUAGE

As we loaded up in Sean's Escalade to head over to the stadium to meet Jason and Coach Shay, I could feel the energy in the group. There's something special about being around elite performers and elite people that makes you want to take your game and life to the next level.

"Hey, Matthew Simonds, everything going OK with you?" Coach Kenny asked. "You look a little down."

"I'm good, Coach," I replied. "Just wondering how I am going to get home and see Erin and the kids."

"Look. There are those who spend their whole life looking for ideal situations and there are those who make the situations they're in ideal," Coach Kenny said. "Be where your feet are. If you are going to be here, your mind might as well be here. Let's make the most out of this day and keep the focus on you making the most of yourself, so that when you get home you will be the best you have ever been for those you care about most."

"You're right, Coach," I responded. "There is nothing I can do but be where my feet are and, as we learned about this morning with the guys, stop feeling sorry for myself."

"Well, Matthew, the first place to start with is your body language. I noticed something had changed in you from the time you walked upstairs to shower till the time you came outside to join us to head to the game," Coach Kenny said. "I can see it in your body language. You gotta get big. Even as you are sitting here, you gotta get big. First you make your body language and then it makes you. Act as if you want to be here and you will get more out of our day and time together than if you wear your emotions on your sleeve. Children do that. Not elite performers."

He was right about that. Michael and Brina wore their emotions on their sleeves. Erin was a rock. She hardly ever changed her emotional state. She was the most consistent person I knew. If she was as upset as she sounded when we talked, I knew I had really let things go and needed to do some significant mending of our relationship at home. I just wasn't sure when that was going to happen. Sooner than later, I hoped.

I knew my body language was terrible. I also knew from talking with the guys about elite mindset that I could change my body language, energy, self-talk, focus [SNAP OF FINGERS] #ThatFast. And I was going to.

CHAPTER 48
AUTOMOBILE UNIVERSITY

"Now connecting. Sean iPhone," the automated voice inside the Escalade said.

Sean's phone had just connected to the Bluetooth in the Escalade and I recognized the voice that came out from the speaker.

"The core of the *Win Forever* philosophy is to compete and do it better than it has ever been done before." It was the voice of Seattle Seahawks head football coach Pete Carroll.

"Oh, excuse me, guys. Let me turn that off," Sean said as he reached for his phone.

"Let that roll, Sean," Chris said from the back of the Escalade.

"Yeah, we are all enrolled in Automobile University. Let it play on," Kyle suggested.

"Hooyah, Sean. Was that Pete Carroll?" David asked.

"No, it's Brian Johnson from the Optimize app. He does Philosophers Notes, just like Cliffs

Notes or Spark Notes on some of the best books out there and he is doing this one on Pete Carroll's book *Win Forever*. Great book," Adam said. "Let that keep playing, Sean."

"Coach Kenny, Matthew Simonds, you cool with listening to this book? Probably be an hour or so till we get to the stadium anyway, we could go through it 3 x, it's only 20minutes long," Sean asked as he made eye contact with me in the rearview mirror with the intensity that only a SEAL could.

"Sean, you know me. I don't even know if the radio in my truck back in Arizona works. All I ever listen to are audio books," Coach Kenny replied. "I have been a huge believer in Automobile University for years. I now look forward to long trips and getting stuck in traffic because it's some of my prime learning time."

"Cool by me, Sean," I answered.

Automobile University. What a great concept. I usually listened to sports talk radio or mindless music when I was driving and typically fell asleep when I would try to read an actual book. Erin was always getting on me about reading and maybe this was how I could do it? Audio books and Philosophers Notes with Brian Johnson.

I was also a huge Pete Carroll fan and was totally impressed with how he turned things around in Seattle and led them to victory in Super Bowl XLVIII, and won back-to-back national titles at The University of Southern California in 2003 and 2004 after being fired five times as a coach.

My boss was always saying "Separation is in preparation" and he attributed that to Coach Carroll.

If we were going to be heading to a PFL game on Thanksgiving, we might as well learn along the way from one of the game's greatest coaches.

CHAPTER 49
THE DRIVE

As we drove to the stadium and listened to the *Win Forever* Philosophers Note on repeat, Sean would routinely stop the audio and lead a discussion about how people were applying the principles that Coach Carroll was teaching to their lives.

Most of our discussion came back to elite mindset, leadership, culture and his *One Play at a Time* system. A lot of what Coach Carroll was talking about was also part of *The 10 Pillars of Mental Performance Mastery*, I wondered if he was MPM certified.

"He spoke about, knowing who you are, what you believe and what you really want. To have a mission, vision and core principles that drive your behavior and decision making.

"You know, guys. When you talk about leadership and culture, I think the process is the same whether you are talking about coaching a football team, leading a company, building a business, leading a SEAL team or leading a family. The process is the same," Coach Kenny said.

"My experience in Mental Performance Mastery and optimal living has shown me that the procedure for creating an MVP process for yourself and your organization is huge. It can also happen in a lot of different ways. The easiest way I have experienced is by starting with some essential elite questions that we all must answer and then by going through a process with yourself and your team to cement your leadership and the culture MVP process that serves as the foundation for you or your team. Is it cool if I ask you guys a couple of elite questions?"

"Hooyah, Coach Kenny," the 5 SEALs said in unison as if it had been planned for them to do so.

I felt like I was riding inside of a motivational seminar and knew that what was about to be discussed was going to be critical to my development. I took out my phone and turned on the voice recorder. I wanted to be sure to remember Coach Kenny's questions and recalled him saying that the power of influence and impact lies in the question asker and that asking the right questions would lead you to the right results.

"Questions help you to make decisions and decisions determine your destiny," Coach Kenny stated. "Nobody ever has or ever will escape the destiny of their decisions. You also never know how the world can be changed by just one decision. The decision on who you will marry, of what school to attend, of what pitch to throw, the decision to gamble, to drink and drive, on what book to grab off the shelf – all of these decisions lead you to your destiny.

"The Boston Red Sox finished dead last in the American League East in 2012, made the decision to hire a new manager and made some minor roster changes, and in 2013 they won the World Series. Before I ask you the critical elite questions, I want to show you how a decision to charge forward regardless of how you feel can literally change the world and reinforce how the decisions that you make today can have far-reaching impact on your children and their children. The decisions we make today can affect generations yet unborn."

As he said this, Coach Kenny turned to look at me. I think he was trying to relay the importance of the decisions that I made. The decision to be with these guys on the way to the game. The decision as to how I was going to get back in the good graces of my wife and kids. And the decision I needed to make to get off the treadmill of life, live more intentionally, be where my feet were, and the decision to be a better person.

CHAPTER 50
FIX YOUR BAYONETS AND CHARGE

Coach Kenny sat up straight in his seat, lifted his hands off his chest, and with open hands and his fingers spread wide he flipped the switch and went into story teller mode. He had the eyes of every man in the Escalade on him... except Sean. Luckily his eyes were on the road.

"Gentlemen, there comes a time in everyone's life when a decision is required. And that decision will have a far-reaching effect on your future. One decision can change your World, and The World. It was July 2, 1863, a hot and humid day, and a schoolteacher from Maine was in the fight of his life.

"Joshua Chamberlain, 34-year-old colonel for the Union Army. The place? Gettysburg, Pennsylvania. He was trying to hold their ground against General Lee's Army of Northern Virginia. After five bloody attacks, his troops realized they wouldn't be able to hold them off any longer.

"More than half his regiment was dead. Of the remaining soldiers, many were wounded. Outnumbered 5 to 1, their last skirmish was done face to face and they were somehow able to push the Confederate Army down the hill. As they surveyed their ammunition, they had less than two bullets per man. For all intents and purposes, they were out of ammunition.

"Glancing downhill and seeing the Confederate attackers ready themselves for their final assault, the other officers tried to talk Chamberlain into retreating.

"They outnumber us, and we have nothing left with which to fight. It's hopeless!" Coach Kenny said as he changed his voice to represent that of one of Chamberlain's men speaking to him.

"Joshua Chamberlain stood silent for a moment.

"Here they come, Sir," Coach Kenny shouted, representing a sergeant yelling to Chamberlain.

"Chamberlain didn't respond as he calculated the cost of freezing, remaining still and staying where he was. The cost was the same as running away.

"Joshua! Joshua, give an order!" Coach Kenny hollered, impersonating Chamberlain's 1st lieutenant and brother Tom screaming on the battlefield.

At this point you could feel the tension in the vehicle. Coach Kenny was a superb storyteller and stories are one of the best ways to teach because they create pictures and our brain works in pictures. We were all sitting on the edge of our seats.

"Chamberlain knew he was not put on this earth to fail," Coach Kenny said.

"We move forward or we die! Fix your bayonets and charge!" Coach Kenny screamed, representing the sure intensity and confidence that Chamberlain must have had.

"As the men fixed their bayonets, Chamberlain pulled out his sword and jumped to the top of the wall. With the enemy less than 50 yards away he screamed, 'Charge! Charge!'

With that decision, the twentieth Maine Regiment poured over the wall and followed a schoolteacher to history. The South, stunned by the aggression and surely thinking that they must have gotten reinforcement, got scared and retreated. Now without any ammo,

Chamberlain and his men captured the entire regiments of the 15th AL and the 47th AL, more than 400 men," Coach Kenny said.

"Of course, it all happened because one man made a decision to CHARGE. And that one decision changed the mindsets of those under his leadership and that decision literally changed the world," Coach Kenny commented. "Confederate troops had taken Ft. Sumter, Richmond, Chancellorsville and Fredericksburg. Had the South won in Gettysburg, many historians believe the war would have been over by the end of the summer. The Confederate States were one victory from winning the war, but they didn't win because an ordinary man, a schoolteacher from Maine, made a decision to move forward and fight.

"We all have decisions to make. What to eat, what to drink, where to invest our time. The challenge is we never know how the decisions that we make are going to impact the future, so often we just make them half-hearted without much intention."

"Hooyah, Coach Kenny," Sean said. "Heck of a story. Chamberlain was a stud! Can you imagine fighting like that? I love how that story shows how one decision can impact the world.

"I think one of the best decisions I ever made in my life was to decide who I wanted to be and to start living a principle-based life vs. a preference-based life," Sean continued. "That decision has made a huge difference for me as a leader on the battle field and as the CEO or Protector Brewery and Burger."

"How did you know what principles to pick as the ones for the foundation of your life, Sean?" I asked.

"Great question, Matthew Simonds," Sean replied. "It wasn't easy and it took me some time. I am now more aware of a process that you can use and it's one that I use when deciding on who to hire to work with me in the Protector Brewery and Burger restaurants I own. I will share this process with you and the guys. I think it's so powerful because it's so simple in execution, and we all need to do simple better. Making the determination that you are going to live a principle-based life actually makes your decision making much easier. Although you might not always like the outcome, it will be easier to live with yourself."

I needed to improve as a leader. I needed to get clarity on my principles and start creating the culture I wanted with my family.

CHAPTER 51
MORE ELITE QUESTIONS

"I love that story, Coach Kenny," I said. "I now realize the importance of being intentional with the decisions that we make and how much the decisions I make will impact my ability to lead and impact my life, my wife, my kids and those I serve."

"Matthew Simonds, don't think you are alone in not having the clarity you want to have on who you are, what you believe and what you want. I have been there, my friend, and go back there on occasion."

"Me too, man," David said.

"Roger that!" Adam agreed.

"Ditto!" Chris said.

"Been there, my man," Kyle added.

"We have all been there, Matthew Simonds," Sean said. "Coach Kenny, what's that process that you used to always take us through in college to help us intentionally grow as leaders individually and grow our culture?"

"The elite questions for leadership and culture?" Coach Kenny asked.

"Yes. The questions." Sean beamed. "They changed my life. We used those when you came in to work with us and I also used them with the SEAL teams I led, with my family, and now with the Protector Brewery and Burgers I own. Can you review those with us as we drive? They changed my life and really helped me get clarity on my leadership and culture."

"As leaders, we need to be good at asking the right questions," Coach Kenny said. "You have to start by asking yourself:

1. If I had three days left to live, what would I do?
2. What do I really want?
3. Who do I need to become to get there?

"Remember, success is something that you attract by becoming a successful person. All successful people have a scoreboard that they evaluate their performance on and part of that scoreboard is knowing who you are. The scoreboard is going to help you with motivation and commitment, focus and awareness, self-control and discipline and time management and organization because measurement is motivation and measurement brings clarity to how productive you have been." Coach Kenny explained. "Matthew Simonds, if you had three days left to live, what would you do?"

I was afraid he was going to ask me that. I had no idea. My initial thoughts were to go bass fishing on Lake Champlain in Vermont where I used to vacation as a kid and where Erin and I went to college, to go get in the front row of a Metallica concert, and to be on a stage teaching a MPM seminar, even though I wasn't certified yet, I knew this was something that I was going to pursue.

I had a pit in my stomach that I did not immediately think of my wife and kids, although I would for sure want them all on the fishing trip, Erin with me at the concert and them all in the audience as I was teaching the MPM seminar. It just felt like something inside of me was missing.

"I'm not sure, Coach," I replied. "If I had three days left to live, I would invest as much time as I could holding my wife and kids, but at this point I am not sure they would want to spend three days with me."
"Sean, what would you do?" Coach Kenny asked.

"I would spend three days giving as much value to the lives of others as possible. I would be with my wife and kids the entire time and I would want to go out serving my country and serving others. My life is about service. Service is one of my core principles, along with self-control, insane work ethic, leadership, vision and adaptability.," Sean answered. "I call it SILVA (service and self-control, insane work ethic, vision, leadership and adaptability. I would want to live my last three days modeling SILVA at the highest level, and I hope I am doing that today, living my life today as if there were three days left. Serving others and modeling SILVA, educating, empowering and energizing others to be the best versions of themselves."

"Matthew Simonds, let me ask you this," Coach Kenny said as he put his hand on my shoulder. "Let's imagine that instead of going to a football game today we were going to a banquet and that banquet was in your honor. All of your friends, family and people who are important in your life are going to be at this banquet. After a meal of grilled chicken and soggy salad like they have at almost every banquet, someone who you choose will stand up and talk about you, your legacy, the impact you had on others, the type of person you are and how you left this world a better place. What would you want them to say at that banquet?"

"That's a great question, Coach," I responded. "I think I would want people to talk about how I was a great husband, a great father, a world-class teacher of MPM and a coach who gave everything he had to help improve the lives of others. Someone who was disciplined with his daily habits and actions. Someone who made a selfless commitment to others and was a great friend and teammate. Someone who had a relentless positive energy like you do, Coach Kenny. Someone who was progressive and always trying to get better at everything he did and at the same time was committed to excellence and being at his best all the time. Above all, I think I would like to be a man of integrity."

"Hooyah, Matthew Simonds!" Sean exclaimed. "Sounds like the start of some core principles and an MVP process you can lead from and build a culture around."

"Good work, Matthew Simonds," Coach Kenny said. "Now the key is to take how you want to be spoken about at your banquet and live that way today. It's time to get intentional about who you are and how you are going to show up, and it's time to stop counting the days and start making the days count. It's time to stop just participating in life and it's time to start dominating in life.

"We have a statement we use in my Inner Circle coaching group and MPM Mastermind and it's called *Dominate the Day! Dominate the Day* is a total commitment to and focus on the moment and what you are doing. It's living this day like it's your last or like you will live forever (your philosophical choice) and living it at the highest level of service to others while taking care of yourself. You can't serve others at the highest level if you are not the best version of you that you have ever been, and to be the best version of you that you have ever been you have to identify who you are going to be. Nobody wants your B game, and if you are not the best you that you have ever been, the best that you can give others is your B game.

"In my Inner Circle and MPM Mastermind which are people who have been through *The 10 Pillars of Mental Performance Mastery Certification* and are committed to living and teaching the pillars, we all work together to raise our boats and bring our A game to the world. Look, high water raises all boats, and in the Inner Circle and MPM Mastermind we raise the water higher than in any other mental performance coaching group on the planet."

I needed to get some of that, but first I needed to get clarity on my own core principles. I wasn't sure if those were going to be my personal core principles, but it sure felt good to talk about and define what I wanted people to say about me at my banquet.

Coach Kenny was right. I needed to, or should I say, wanted to lock down my core principles and start Dominating the Days! I was 100% on cruise control in life and I was now as sure as ever that I was heading in the wrong direction.

Meeting Coach Kenny was helping me to re-route back to being the best version of me that I had ever been.

CHAPTER 52
THE STADIUM

We had been driving for just about an hour and were pulling into the stadium where the fans looked like they had been tailgating for days.

People were roasting turkey, others were playing cornhole, and dads were tossing the pigskin with their children. I vowed to never let another Thanksgiving go by where I did not toss the pigskin with Michael and Brina and have a bite of turkey with them and Erin.

As Sean pulled into a VIP parking lot, a man ran out and dove across the Escalade hood like he was sliding into home plate head first. He looked like Eric Byrnes, the MLB analyst's twin brother, only not as much energy as Byrnes brought to the network.

"Must be Jason," one of the SEALs said. "That guy's the most juiceful dude I have ever met and a bit crazy."

As we parked, Sean exploded out of the vehicle like a man on a mission and gave Jason a HUGE hug. As the two embraced, I could only imagine the bond that these two former SEAL teammates and college football teammates must have had through their time together. It was special to be a part of it.

After reconnecting with Sean, the SEALs and Coach Kenny, Jason shook my hand and said how excited he was to have the chance to meet me. I thanked him for the opportunity to be at the game and to meet Coach Shay. At that moment, he looked down at his watch and said that Coach was waiting for us and excited to meet us, and that we had to roll out quickly before the team had to take to the field for warm-ups if we were going to *'get some'* with coach Shay.

And with that we all walked from the parking lot towards the stadium. There was a buzz in the air, not only about the game, but with the group I was with to go and meet the hottest name in coaching, Tony Shay, head coach of The Detroit Dominators.

CHAPTER 53
MEETING COACH SHAY

As we walked through the main players' entrance towards the locker room at a quick pace, I remembered what Coach Kenny had said one time about successful people walking 20% faster because they had a healthy sense of urgency and were on a mission to serve. Following Jason, I felt like we were sprinting.

The energy around the stadium was tremendous. As we made it past security, Jason told us to look to the right, and on the wall was a sign that read:

> *Welcome to DETROIT. Home of the Dominators. Through this gate walk people of DISCIPLINE who are committed to EXCELLENCE, who compete with TOUGHNESS and a RELENTLESS energy ONE PLAY AT A TIME and work with INTENSITY and INTEGRITY TOGETHER... WE ARE... DETROIT!*

It was clear. Tony Shay had implemented a principle-driven philosophy in his leadership with the Dominators and they were seeing the results; being undefeated at Thanksgiving in high school football was difficult, let alone against the best players in the world in the PFL.

As we walked further into the stadium, Jason stopped, turned to all of us, and made us get in a huddle. With all of our arms around each other, he made eye contact with each of us.

"Men, you are about to meet one of the best coaches in the world and one of the most influential people in my life. Coach Shay is a living example of *The 10 Pillars of Mental Performance Mastery*. He and his entire staff are MPM certified coaches and the results are evident. They live these pillars daily in all they do. He is the best at coaching *The 10 Pillars of Mental Performance Mastery* I have ever been around and is also second to none in training an elite mindset (Pillar #1) in his players and in leading (Pillar #9) his staff and this organization to build the right culture (Pillar #10).

"He is one of the most motivated and committed (Pillar #2) people I know. His focus and awareness (Pillar #3) are off the charts. He puts the process first (Pillar #5) and the outcome second; and as you can tell, he gets a lot of outcome. He has tremendous self-control and discipline (Pillar #4), has a vision and creates that vision by using meditation and mental imagery (Pillar #6) with his team on a daily basis. He knows that everything happens twice – first you have to believe it and then you will see it, while the competition always thinks first you have to see it and then you will believe it. He is an over-achiever and an over-believer, but most of all he is a strategist and he lives *The 10 Pillars of Mental Performance Mastery* and demands that his staff and players do as well. It's easy; they just model what he does with his routines and habits of excellence (Pillar #7). He also has some of the best time management and organizational skills (Pillar #8) of anyone I have ever met.

"When it's time to leave our meeting, he will let us know. Don't feel like you have to watch the clock. He has that taken care of. At the end, he will want us all to break it down with him like he does with his team, so I want you guys to know how," Jason said.

"He will ask you to put your left hand in, because your left hand is closer to your heart. Coach Shay believes that how you do anything is how you do everything, and if you are going to do anything you must put your heart into it. He will also ask that you go palm up because we will need to lift each other up in life if we are going to make it to the top. Then he will have you say *DETROIT* on *One* to reinforce the core principles you saw on the wall on the way into the stadium.

He will have you do it on *One* because he wants to be first in everything. He will also know your name and will be the first to extend his hand to you, so don't be caught off guard, be prides himself on being first."

As we all put our left hands in and broke on *DETROIT* on *One*, I was blown away at how intentional they were. Even the way they broke the team huddle was intentional. I loved how they broke on *One*. It pays to be a winner – and when you think about it, why would you reinforce any other number?

As we walked a little further, we turned the corner and there was Tony Shay, the head coach of the Detroit Dominators.

Coach Shay was about 6'2", 200lbs and in great shape. He was cleanly shaven with a tight haircut and had a can of Red Bull in his hand. He had a presence to him that reminded me of what a younger Coach Kenny must have been like: intense, intentional, extremely present and positive.

"Jason, my man. So good to see you," he exclaimed as he gave his former player a big 20 second hug. "Coach Kenny, Sean, Chris, Kyle,

Adam, David, Matthew Simonds," he said as he reached out to shake all of our hands as if he had met us before and known us his entire life. "It's great to have you here with us. Welcome to Detroit. Let's head into the office and break down some of *The 10 Pillars of Mental Performance Mastery*, shall we?"

Jason was right; he knew all of our names and was the definition of "on top of it."

As we walked down the hall towards his office, you could hear loud music playing. The song "Seal the Deal" by Volbeat was pumping in the weight room at a deafening level as a group of what looked like coaches pumped out some pull-ups, push-ups and body weight squats while another group was hammering bicep curls in the mirror.

"The staff likes to get a pump in before the game following the Arm Farm program," Coach Shay said with a smile. "They also do The Murph and then Surf the Rack hitting the biceps for a max on every dumbbell starting at the heaviest and working down. It's a real pump. They listen to that song you hear and 'A Warrior's Call' by Volbeat on repeat.

It's B-E-A-U-tiful. I got mine in earlier so I could meet with you guys or I'd be in there getting some with them."

As I looked into the room, I saw that the same words used in the sign on the way into the facility were also displayed on the columns in the weight room:

Discipline
Excellence
Toughness
Relentless
One Play at a Time
Intensity & Integrity
Together

As we walked past the players' locker room, we saw the same sign on the walls in there as well, with graphics of the best Dominators players in action shots behind each of the words.

We finally made it to Coach Shay's office and sat down at his D-shaped conference table, and engraved in the D were the same core principles.

Their core principles were everywhere. The same exact sign that was on the wall as we walked into the stadium was on his wall.

"Gentlemen, Jason told me that you wanted to know how we are having so much success this season. I will tell you. Success doesn't happen by accident; it happens by intention," Coach Shay said. "Let me ask you this. You have been here for five minutes. Do you know why we are successful yet?"

CHAPTER 54
BE CONSISTENT AND INTENTIONAL

"The reason why we are successful is really simple. We are consistent and intentional about everything we do, and everything we do is tied back to *The 10 Pillars of Mental Performance Mastery* system that you have been learning about with Coach Kenny, is that right? That's what Jason told me you guys have been doing this morning."

"Yes sir, that's correct," I said. "It's been amazing."

"In the past, this organization didn't know how to help their players and coaches develop the mental performance mastery skillset that it takes to consistently be at their best, reach their goals, build leaders within the right culture and achieve long-term success. We have implemented *The 10 Pillars of Mental Performance Mastery*, a proven system that teaches you how.

"Let me review this for you."

PILLAR #1 ELITE MINDSET

"We are intentional about how we train the elite mindset of our players. Many coaches can't seem to get the people they coach to be responsible for bringing consistent energy to their workouts, to stay positive when things get hard, and to understand that they can grow and train your mindset just like they do their body. We can.

PILLAR #2 MOTIVATION AND COMMITMENT

"We are intentional about helping the people in our organization increase their motivation and commitment for the journey and the work it takes to be great. Most people are not consistently focused and committed to a clear goal and a why, so they lose motivation. Our players and staff are very clear with their why.

PILLAR #3 FOCUS AND SELF-AWARENESSS

"We are intentional in helping them develop the focus and self-awareness it takes to be an elite performer. If you don't have present-moment focus and self-awareness, you won't be able to navigate the adversity that is part of the game and you won't perform at your best on a consistent basis.

PILLAR #4 SELF-CONTROL AND DISCIPLINE
"We are intentional about relentlessly working to help our players develop the self-control and discipline it takes to put off what they want in the moment for what they want most. If you aren't in control of yourself within a situation, you can't make the most effective decisions, and it's our decisions that determine our destiny in sports and in life. Our players live in a world of distraction; helping them to manage those distractions and process them properly is one of the keys of our success.

PILLR #5 PROCESS OVER OUTCOME
"We are intentional about putting the process over the outcome because when you focus on outcome, you lose sight of the process it takes to achieve it. Results are real and the process is the pathway to get results. Since we don't focus on the outcome, we actually get better results. Most people don't get that – they are too fixated on the outcome because pride and ego get in the way of the humility it takes to achieve the desired results.

PILLAR #6 MENTAL IMAGERY AND MEDITATION
"We take them through daily mental imagery and meditation processes, so they are working on their mental game every day. Most of the

players didn't understand the power of mental imagery and how images that you create (both positive and negative) have a direct impact on your physical and mental performance. The players here in Detroit were not intentionally visualizing their performance because they either didn't know how to visualize or did not understand its importance.

PILLAR #7 ROUTINES AND HABITS OF EXCELLENCE
"To help them with a lack of consistency in preparation, performance and results, we are super intentional about creating the routines and habits of excellence they need to perform on a consistent basis.

PILLAR #8 TIME MANAGEMENT AND ORGANIZATION
"We also take a lot of time to help them with their time management and organizational skills. In the past, I couldn't get the people I coached to do what I wanted them to do outside of practice so that the work we did in practice could keep progressing them. If we can't get our players or if you can't get your clients to be organized, to plan their time and stick to their plan because they don't have the time management and organizational skills they need, all of the previous pillars will not be at the right levels and you will lose.

PILLAR #9 LEADERSHIP
"We are intentional about teaching the leadership skills that our players need to build trust with their teammates and to get the results that we want on and off the field. Many of the coaches on my staff have said that in the past they couldn't get the people they coached to develop the leadership skills they needed so that they could help create the right culture and achieve both their individual and team performance goals.

PILLAR #10 THE RIGHT CULTURE
"We are intentional about creating a culture here in DETROIT! A lot of my coaching friends can't seem to get their players and staff to buy into their culture, to take ownership of and live their organizational mission, vision and core principles. We have that happening right now and it's special and by design.

"We don't have a ton of time today men, but I wanted to lift the curtain so you could see what we do, how we do it and why we are winning," Coach Shay said. "I'm glad you are here with me today, men. How can I best serve you in the limited time we have together?"

CHAPTER 55
GOING A LITTLE DEEPER WITH
THE 10 PILLARS OF MENTAL PERFORMANCE MASTERY

I couldn't write fast enough. Coach Shay not only had a clear mission for his organization, he was a man on a mission implementing *The 10 Pillars of Mental Performance Mastery* in his life and in his organization, and it was evident.

"Coach Shay, it's obvious that you are intentional and consistent about everything that you feel is important to the success of your organization," Coach Kenny said. "Would you be willing to go a little deeper on how you apply each of the pillars here with The Detroit Dominators?"

PILLAR #1 ELITE MINDSET
"Of course," Coach Shay said. "Elite mindset is always where we start. Your mindset is your perspective; it's how you see yourself, your situation and the world. We want our players to have an elite mindset and a growth mindset. We believe that an elite and growth mindset is at the foundation of player development and one of our greatest skillsets.

PILLAR #2 MOTIVATION AND COMMITMENT

"To keep our organizational motivation and commitment high, we like to advertise the mentality and the culture we want in our people. At every weekly meeting, we recognize those who have intentionally lived our core principles and we ask people to stand up who have achieved a step in their vision. And we CELEBRATE that.

"Without goals and a vision, the people will perish. We get lost when we have no direction. We call those goals either our personal or organizational vision and when we achieve a step in the vision, either as an organization or individually, we want to recognize that.

"We also measure everything. We have people who measure how many high fives we give, how many people we escort to their seat, how many tackles for a loss we have and, of course, how many points we get. There is a lot that goes into getting points, and we like to measure the process because we feel like that motivates our players and employees for more process – and rewarded behavior is repeated behavior.

"The process is the pathway to results, and results – goal or vision achievement – are what will increase the motivation and commitment of our organization.

"We also have a *why* wall where everyone shares why they choose to be a part of this organization. Our coaches share why they coach and/or players share why they play. We also share what we want to each individually get out of being a part of the Dominators. There isn't a day that goes by where someone won't ask you about your why or what you want. We believe that when you have a big enough reason why you will always find a way how.

PILLAR #3 FOCUS AND AWARENESS
"When we have motivation and commitment, we then start working on the focus and awareness of our organization. We want our players and employees to have a high level of focus on the moment, a focus on being where their feet are, on giving the greatest gift they can give – their presence. We also want them to know that every day isn't going to be sunshine and roses. Hell, this is Detroit, not Disney, there are any unicorns farting fairy dust around here with t-shirts on that say be positive. There is a formula, present, process productive. Look, there are going to be hard times, bad plays, upset guests

and fans that we need to work with to get back into a green light.

"We use a signal light analogy to help people understand awareness. If you are in control and going good, you are in green. When you start to lose control, you go into yellow and when you lose control, you are in red lights. We are never going to eliminate yellow and red lights; we just want to get better at managing them and work to be in green as much as we can.

"Awareness is critical because awareness is the precursor to all change. With awareness, you can change; without it you will be the victim of your emotions or a victim of your circumstances.

PILLAR #4 SELF-CONTROL AND DISCIPLINE
"A lot of our players think that playing football out of emotion helps them, but it actually hurts them. We need them to play out of a one-play-at-a-time process and stay in control of their emotions. Present, process, productive.

"We teach that you have to be in control of yourself before you can control your performance, and that you have very little control of what goes on around you, but total control of how you choose to respond to it.

PILLAR #5 PROCESS OVER OUTCOME

"Being able to use this awareness and focus on the moment is all part of our *process over outcome* approach. Everyone wants the outcome, but it's the process that's the pathway to the outcome. And using the KISS principle, Keep It Super Simple, we say that the process is about controlling what you can control and keeping your eyes fixed on the microscope goals you have. If you execute this day to day, you will achieve your telescope goals or the goals that you have in your future.

"Once we have clarity on the process, then we really work to build the skills of self-control and discipline. Our players know what's right and wrong, yet they still get caught up in the moment and put off what they want most for what they want in the moment.

"This year they have done a great job in discipline and staying in process, where in the past we have struggled. We have had players that once they won 2-3 games in a row, they started to let their guard down and let the attention to detail slip. This is why we emphasize that all of our players make their bed and keep their lockers organized a certain way.

"We had an Admiral from the US Navy come in and speak to our organization about this. You would be amazed at how the simple act of making your bed can set you up for a successful day and how not making your bed can be a sign that you are dropping your guard on detail – and in our sport when one guy drops his guard on detail, the other 10 suffer."

"Hooyah, Coach Shay!" Sean exclaimed. "I've been making my bed since boot camp – haven't missed a day. I even do it in hotels... even on the days I check out."

"Roger that," Jason agreed. "Made mine today."

"So, did I, men," Coach Shay said. "We use that same principle in our weight room and locker room. When we put weights away, we always put the **D** on the plates and on the dumbbells up so that you can clearly see the D. I picked that up from a giant in the strength coaching industry and a master of *The 10 Pillars of Mental Performance Mastery*, Dr. Tru. We actually sat next to each other during our MPM certification and have stayed in contact for years after in the Inner Circle and MPM Mastermind.

"This is a detail that we want our guys to focus on when they are tired and fatigued in training so they can focus on the details in competition. It's all part of our process and part of our checks and balances for discipline and self-control. We have even gone as far as having a chocolate cake in the dining room at all times... If a player gets close to taking a slice, his teammates are on him like feathers on a goose. The leaders on the team said they wanted the cake in there as a temptation to their discipline and said that they will only eat it on the days that we win.

"We now have HUGE chocolate cakes in the shape of a **D** in the locker room after we win. I tell you what, men. Cake has NEVER tasted so good as it does after a win! You will see players on the field today making a motion like they are feeding themselves after a sack or a tackle for a loss. This is all about reminding guys that we want to win so we can crush that cake. It's been a lot of fun for the guys, and I will keep feeding them cake as long as we keep winning. It's been a fun reward for their efforts."

"What do you do with the cake if you lose?" I asked.

"Well, Matthew Simonds… we haven't lost yet, so don't jinx us," Coach Shay said as he glared at me with the intensity of a professional football league coach. "Just kidding. We believe in process and execution, not luck and superstition. If we lose, we will select a player of the game, because even in a loss there are guys who will play extremely well, and that player then will get to take the cake and deliver it to a local shelter for the less fortunate or bring it to a children's hospital.

"It's something that will help them to get over the loss quickly and something that the players will realize as a life-changing experience. So, even in defeat, we will build better people and win championships in the community of Detroit.

"When we win the world championship, we will have the biggest cake party in the history of the world. We will have a D-shaped cake the size of the **D** at the middle of the field, and we will have the players serve the fans and thank them for all of their support. It will be the single greatest day in the history of this organization. I have seen this celebration party over and over in my head. We will get to serve our fans – and a day without service is a day not lived. I can see this vision clearly and I have shared that vision with our players and staff. It's funny how they all now will send me selfies from birthday parties and post photos in Instagram of them not eating cake but serving it to others as practice for when we win the last game."

All of a sudden there was a knock on the door.

"Coach Shay, five minutes till team meeting," a man who had popped into Coach Shay's office said and then spun around and left just as fast as he walked in.

"Well men, let's finish up," Coach Shay said. "Let's talk about mental imagery and meditation.

PILLAR #6 MENTAL IMAGERY AND MEDITATION
"We do mental imagery and meditation every day, either as a team or as individuals. The difference is that mental imagery is specifically experiencing yourself doing a certain action like playing or coaching football, while doing meditation is about quieting and clearing your mind.

"One of my assistant coaches, Kevin Guzzo, shared with me that there are 1,440 minutes in a day and that 1% of 1,440 minutes is 14:40. We made our mental imagery and meditation audios that are on each of our players' phones

14:40 so that when we say our focus is on getting 1% better today, what we really mean is that for 1% of our day we are truly working on Mental Performance Mastery when our opponents are not. We call this our 1% MPM advantage.

"Some of our players breathe using a routine of 6-2-8 for 14:40, some do a 5x5 box breathing exercise, and some mix it up. We have a kicker from Amsterdam named Rick Vadenkurk that does the Ice Man Breathing Method that he brought with him from his time in The Netherlands and Japan. It's fascinating.

"Some of our players do the mental imagery more and others do the meditation more. The goal is that they do one or the other for 1% of their day 5-7 days a week. This breath work and quieting of the mind helps them on the field as well.

PILLAR #7 ROUTINES AND HABITS OF EXCELLENCE
"We make a huge teaching emphasis on routines and habits of excellence. First, we create our habits and then our habits create us. We become what we do on a routine basis.

"Our coaches work with the players in their unit rooms to create AM and PM routines and also pre-and post-play and pre-and post competition routines. When you watch today, you will see each player take a deep breath before the snap. This pre-play routine ties directly back to their meditation and mental imagery practice, in that they have conditioned themselves like snipers – when they take that full belly breath, they are slowing their heart rate down and getting into the present for that shot or for that play."

"We have a former Navy SEAL named Chris "Lav" Lavoie on our staff and he works with our guys a lot on breathing and slowing yourself down so that you can slow the game down. You guys may have seen him on *The Selection* from The History Channel? If you have not seen it, you are missing out. Watch it!"

"Hooyah, Coach Shay," Sean said. "I was at BUD/S with Lav. As quality of a dude as you will find. My son's football team all watched *The Selection* together and had Lav do a Skype call with them. My son told me that was the highlight of his 2017. Has he had your guys do the 1,000 sit-ups that he did on the show?"

"Funny you mention that, Sean," Coach Shay replied with a smile. "We have two guys on our staff that do the 1,000 sit-ups challenge every game day as part of their routine. They are animals. They do The Murph then they Surf the Rack doing as many bicep curls as possible, starting with as heavy a weight as they can lift to get one and then working down to the 5lb weights, rep out The Arm Farm And then they do the 1,000 sit-ups. They are in the weight room for like 4 hours on game day getting a serious pump in, locking in their energy and focus and getting their minds right.

"Lav talks with our guys about one play at a time and the 10 pillars. He has a book coming out about it that we will use with the team next year. It will be great.

"I don't want to spoil what his book is all but I will tell you that it reinforces much of *The 10 Pillars of Mental Performance Mastery* beautifully.
"He walked our guys through the visualization process he used as a Navy SEAL sniper and then, next thing you know, all of our guys are wanting him to make them custom mental imagery audios, which he did following a simple five-step process.

"It's been HUGE for our guys. He will actually work with us in the hotel the night before games. Our strength staff will put the team through a short yoga flex routine and then Lav will take them through a mental imagery session of the game the next day. It's been awesome. We have players and coaches on our team that have had him make these audios for their kids who are athletes. I don't know how he does it all."

"Lav was with us last night in the hotel and is flying back to Arizona today after the game to teach a MPM certification course for coaches and trainers. He is actually flying back with our owner, Dr. Rob, after the game. Dr. Rob is a former sport psychology professor from a school in New Jersey and hit it big with his books and online training programs. He just bought the team two years ago. Needless to say, Dr. Rob is all about *The 10 Pillars of Mental Performance Mastery*. He is actually going to sit in on the certification course that Lav is teaching so he can be MPM certified like all of our coaches. He has been to like almost every one of the seminars that Lav has taught. Dr. Rob is awesome. It's refreshing having an owner that actually gets it."

Flying back to Arizona after the game... Man, I thought if I only could get on that plane with Lav and Dr. Rob, I could get back in time on Thanksgiving Day and for my wife's birthday.

That would be amazing.

CHAPTER 56
IF YOU DON'T ASK, THE ANSWER IS ALWAYS *NO*

"Coach Shay," Coach Kenny said, "I know that if you don't ask, the answer is always *no*. Matthew Simonds and I are here because our flight to Arizona yesterday got canceled. It has worked out for the best; otherwise, we would not have been able to be with Sean and the other SEALs here with us, nor had the chance to meet with you today or go to the game. We are extremely grateful.

"I assume that Lav and Dr. Rob are flying to Arizona on a private jet after the game. Is there any way we can see if there are open seats so that we both may be able to get back home for Thanksgiving?"

"That's a bold ask, Coach Kenny," Coach Shay responded. "If you aren't bold, you ain't living right! Let me ask. How great would that be if you were able to fly back to Arizona after the game with Dr. Rob and Lav and be with your families? I know that Detroit is a zoo this time of year. I know they would both love it. Just be ready for some energy because Lav brings the juice and after games Dr. Rob wants to replay the game, play by play, with anyone who will listen, especially if we win. Let me text my DFE Jacob "El-Chappy-Tan" Armstrong to see if he can make that happen.

"Let me also check Lav's 168 and see where he is – you guys have to meet this man. That is actually a great segue into time management and organization.

PILLAR #8 TIME MANAGEMENT AND ORGANIZATION
"Look, we have been successful this year because we operate out of intention with everything we do. If you are NOT organized and efficient with your time, you can NOT be intentional because you are always behind and always doing what's urgent, rather than doing what's important.

"I have all of my staff keep a 168 on their phones and share it with me through Google Docs so that I can see what they are doing, where they are, and we can all be on the same page and as efficient and effective as possible.

"Time is the great equalizer of all men. Many people complain and use the excuse that they don't have enough time. This is an excuse made by those with an average mindset. It's not that they don't have enough time; they just don't have enough value for their time and enough time management and organization skill to get a lot done in a day. Thus, they get caught up in trying to please everyone and get stressed out most of the time, unable to be productive. Remember, present, process, productive, that is the formula.

"They might feel efficient but are not effective. Efficiency is doing things quickly and effectiveness is doing the right things well. In the world of distraction, it's easy to get sucked into the web or into social media and to go a full day feeling efficient but not being effective.

"To be as effective as possible I want my coaches, and they want their players, to schedule every minute of their days and plan tomorrow tonight. That's one of our mantras that we come back to about time management and organization. Plan tomorrow tonight so you can wake up tomorrow a man on a mission working to accomplish a vision."

Coach Shay then opened up his phone and through Apple AirPlay showed us the screen on his phone on the TV in his office. On it was a 168 for every one of his staff members and players. He clicked on the *Lav 168* file.

What opened was as detailed of a schedule as I have ever seen. Every minute was accounted for. He had scheduled when he was going to sleep, eat, exercise, shower, walk from his office to the field, call his wife, etc. It was all on there.

It was 11:29am and his schedule said that from 11:25-11:30am he was walking to the team meeting room.

Coach Shay immediately spun out of his chair and opened his door. "Lav," he yelled.

Not 10 seconds later a short blond-haired, wide-eyed man full of juice walked into Coach Shay's office. "What's up, bro?" Lav said as he embraced Coach Shay.

"No way. Get the heck out. Sean, what are you doing here?" Lav asked as he walked across the room and gave Sean a hug. "Left arm up, bro, puts us heart to heart. Let's do that hug again. 20 seconds."

These guys were intentional about everything; even the way they hugged had a purpose. They hugged again, this time with the left arm up as to put themselves heart to heart with the person they were hugging.

"Lav, meet former SEALs David, Adam, Kyle, Chris and Jason. Meet my mentor Coach Kenny and my friend Matthew Simonds."

"Hooyah, men!" Lav said as he shook each person's hand and said each person's name.

"Lav, Matthew Simonds and Coach Kenny are trying to get back to Arizona and I figured you were flying there with Dr. Rob. Do you think..."

CHAPTER 57
THE TEXT

Just then Coach Shay received a text back from El-Chappy-Tan his DFE.

"Dr. Rob said and you guys are good to go," Coach Shay said. "Dr. Rob wanted me to tell you guys that you better bring the juice today because if you are juiceful, you are useful and if you are juiceless, you are useless. Dr. Rob is all about the juice.

"Lav, I am going to have you take Coach Kenny and Matthew Simonds and the boys up to Dr. Rob's suite for the game. And then will you make sure that Coach Kenny and Matthew Simonds get back to Arizona tonight so they can have some turkey with their families?"

"Roger that, Coach Shay. Done deal," Lav said.

"I also think you should invite Coach Kenny and Matthew Simonds to *The 10 Pillars of Mental Performance Mastery* certification seminar that you are doing in Arizona this weekend. I think they would really enjoy it and I'd like to sponsor them. Can you make that happen?" Coach Shay asked.

"Roger that also, Coach. I will get them the details on the certification," Lav replied. I will add their names to the insiders list."

"Men, I hope you are able to attend *The 10 Pillars of Mental Performance Mastery* certification course with Lav this weekend in Arizona. I can tell you that we are winning because we are intentional about applying the pillars in everything we do.

"Every team in this league has talent, but talent alone is never enough. You need a certain level of talent to get in the game, but all the teams at this level have talent.

The difference is the 8 pillars we have talked about and the final two.

PILLAR #9 LEADERSHIP
"We also train leadership in our staff and players. We have weekly leadership training – it's optional and everyone shows up. Winning is also optional. It's no surprise that all of our staff and players show up and we are winning.

"In those leadership meetings, we are always teaching the skills of connecting with others, trying to grow their competence in understanding our culture and the importance of displaying their character and living a principle-based life. We believe that you must build trust with those who you go to battle with each Sunday and that we must get results.

"The players and staff are executing the process right now and we are getting results. I get asked all the time, *What comes first – confidence or success?* We believe that confidence comes before success but that trust comes before confidence.

"When there is a high level of trust, our players will have more clarity on what their role is and what we expect of them. With that clarity it becomes easier to hold others accountable and to provide support. We have each person create his own MVP Process and identify his mission, vision and core principles, as we feel that knowing who you are is the foundation of living with character and showing up consistently. We want all of our players and staff to develop leadership qualities and we believe that starts with their MVP process and building trust with each other. We have great leadership and our leadership is responsible for creating the right culture.

PILLAR #10 THE RIGHT CULTURE

"We also discuss on a daily basis what the right culture is for our organization. We have an organizational MVP Process and feel that it's up to the leadership of the organization to share this with the team, then model it and get the players to live by it.

"We believe that leadership is responsible for developing culture and that the purpose of culture is to have a shared purpose which we call a Mission, a shared set of goals we call a Vision, and a shared set of core principles we strive to live by and behave by on a moment to moment basis.

"It's the core principles and those beliefs that drive the behaviors of people in our organization. We are very clear on what behaviors are above the line and will help us to win a world championship and what behaviors are below the line and will keep us from winning a championship. It's those behaviors that we bring every day that will determine our results.

"Our organizational MVP process is:

MISSION: The mission of the Detroit Dominators is to be an elite entertainment and educational organization that represents the city of Detroit with class and championships on and off the field.

VISION: The vision of the Detroit Dominators is to run the best player development program in all of football, to win the opener, win our division, host throughout the playoffs, go to the Super Bowl and win the Super Bowl.

CORE PRINCIPLES:

Discipline: Having a plan and sticking to it.

Excellence: Commitment to growing into your best self.

Toughness: Overcoming any and all adversity.

Relentless: A contagious positive energy to give your all.

One Play at a Time: Being where your feet are and in the now.

Intensity & **I**ntegrity: Extreme focus for always doing what's right and what's right now.

Together: We over me, Dominators first and Dominators last.

"Everyone in our organization then has a plan to help them personally grow called a Start, Stop and Continue (SSC) growth plan.

"Each member of our leadership team is responsible for making sure those who they lead have an SSC because we know that growth does not happen by accident; it only happens by intention. We do it on the team with our position coaches and every one of our employees has an SSC with their managers.

"The head of concessions does it with her team and the head of security does as well. Ask anyone wearing the **D** on their chest what they are working on or what their SSC is and they will be able to tell you.

"We are growing leaders here in our culture and you are seeing the results on the field and in the stadium experience. We all want more wins… and we are now living the process that if you want more, you must become more."

"Coach Shay, I noticed that you had the DETROIT acronym in your office. It was in the hall and in the weight room as well," Coach Kenny stated. "Is that by design?"

"Coach Kenny, I am glad you asked," Coach Shay said as his face lit up. "That same sign is in every room in this stadium. Every office, every bathroom stall, every concession stand. It's everywhere. We as humans are like water; we like to take the easiest path possible and we need a lot of reminders. It's why advertising is so expensive – it works.

"Men, to bring this great meeting to a close, please know that the difference in Detroit this year vs. previous years is the implementation of the 10 pillars of mental performance mastery. The 10 pillars have changed my life, they have changed this organization, and they have helped me to be the best version of myself. They have made me a better coach, a better husband and a better father. I have no doubt they will do the same for you, your family and your career.

"Bring it in, men. We have plays to win," Coach Shay said as he ushered us all into a huddle. "Left hands in, because we put our hearts into what we do and the people we do it with. Palms up, because you have to lift each other up. *DETROIT* on *One*, because we put Detroit first in all we do. 3-2-1... DETROIT!"

CHAPTER 58
THE SUITE

As I sat in Dr. Rob's owner's suite at The Detroit Dominators stadium, I felt like life had been injected into me. From Coach Kenny, Sean and the SEALs, to Coach Shay, Lav and Dr. Rob, who was as nice a guy as you will ever meet, these were elite people. These were leaders, people who were built for others and people who truly were in pursuit of the best version of themselves.

I was also ecstatic that I was going to be able to fly back to Arizona after the game, and on a private jet for that matter.

I was most excited that when I texted Erin that I would be home later tonight she sent back a smiley face emoji and said they would wait for Dad to get home for Thanksgiving. Also, she was quite happy that I found a way home for Thanksgiving and her birthday.

I was excited to get home and mend my relationship with her and the kids.

I was also grateful that Coach Shay was going to sponsor me to get certified in *The 10 Pillars of*

Mental Performance Mastery over weekend so that I truly could become the best version of myself and help others to do the same.

I was, above all, grateful for Coach Kenny and his investment into me and showing me a better way to live, to love and to serve others. That way was through *The 10 Pillars of Mental Performance Mastery*.

ABOUT THE AUTHOR

Brian Cain, MPM, is a #1 best-selling author, speaker and the creator of *The Mental Performance Daily Podcast, The 10 Pillars of Mental Performance Mastery (MPM) System, The MPM Coaches Certification Course* and *The 30 Days To MPM Athletes Program.*

It's his mission to certify 10,000 coaches who each educate, empower and energize more than 1,000 clients so that together they can impact and influence over 10,000,000 lives.

Brian has worked with coaches, athletes, and teams at the Olympic level and in the National Football League (NFL), National Basketball Association (NBA), National Hockey League (NHL), Ultimate Fighting Championship (UFC), on the Professional Golf Tour (PGA) and in Major League Baseball (MLB).

His client list includes 6 former UFC Champions, 4 Major League Baseball Cy Young Award winners, a Heisman Trophy winner and more than 1,000 professional sports draft pics including the #1 overall pick in both the MLB and NFL Draft.

As a coach, Brian personally knows the challenges coaches go through to build their business while also staying committed to being the best version of themselves.

Brian has spoken on stages all over the world and has delivered his keynotes on *The 10 Pillars of Mental Performance Mastery* and *How To Get One Percent Better* at in-service trainings, corporate retreats, leadership summits, and conventions in education, sports and business.

Highly sought after as a speaker and trainer, Brian delivers his message with passion, in an engaging style that keeps his audiences energized, focused and empowered through the learning process.

As someone who lives what he teaches, Brian will inspire you and, more importantly, give you the tools necessary to get the most out of your career and life and close the gap from where you are to where you want to be by living *The 10 Pillars of Mental Performance Mastery.*

START LISTENING TO
THE MENTAL PERFORMANCE DAILY PODCAST

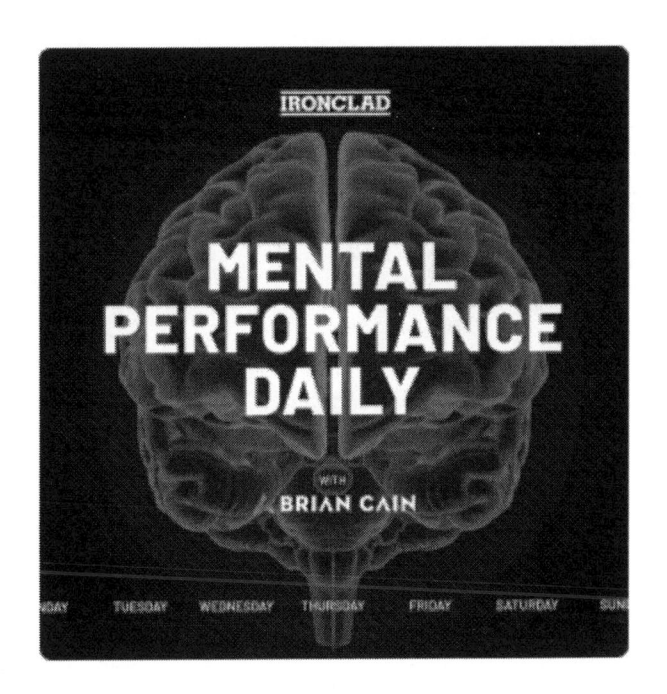

LISTEN TODAY AT
BrianCain.com

BECOME A
MENTAL PERFORMANCE MASTERY
(MPM) CERTIFIED COACH

Want to receive the same training, mentorship and certification Coach Kenny, Tony Shay and Sean The SEAL taught to Matthew Simonds? Become a Brian Cain Peak Performance Certified MPM Coach, start teaching *The 10 Pillars of Mental Performance Mastery* and start having more influence and impact on those you serve while increasing your income doing work you love.

**JOIN THE INSIDERS LIST
TO SAVE $200 & LEARN MORE AT
BrianCain.com/certification**

BECOME A
MENTAL PERFORMANCE MASTERY
(MPM) TRAINED ATHLETE

Want to receive the same training that Coach Kenny uses with his clients and that Brian Cain uses with the professional collegiate and high school athletes he mentors, including 6 UFC World Champions, a Heisman Trophy Winner, NFL MVP, NFL Rookie of The Year and 4 MLB Cy Young Award Winners?

LEARN MORE AND JOIN OTHER TOP ATHLETES AT
BrianCain.com/athletes

TEAM CONSULTING

Brian offers team consulting packages to help you facilitate his *10 Pillars of Mental Performance Mastery System* and his world class experience as a consultant, let Brian help you close the gap from where are to where you want to be.

LEARN MORE AT
BrianCain.com/consulting

KEYNOTE SPEAKING

Brian delivers his message with energy, engagement, and enthusiasm to help educate, empower, and energize his audiences. If you are looking for a keynote speaker who will energize your team/staff and leave them with simple and powerful tools to transform their lives and the lives of those they lead, contact Brian today.

LEARN MORE AT
BrianCain.com/speaking

1-1 COACHING

Brian works one-on-one with teachers, students, coaches, athletes, and executives in applying *The 10 Pillars of Mental Performance Mastery*.

He is now offering one-on-one coaching opportunities where he can work with you directly to apply the information in this book to your life so that you can close the gap from where you are to where you want to be.

LEARN MORE AT
BrianCain.com/coaching

CONNECT WITH BRIAN

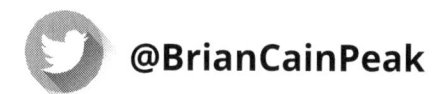

@BrianCainPeak

/BrianCainPeak

/BrianCainPeak

/BrianCainPeak

@BrianCainPeak

CONTACT BRIAN BY VISITING
BrianCain.com/contact

WHERE'S BRIAN?

Find out when Brian will be in your area and inquire about having him come speak with you and your team, school or organization!

VIEW BRIAN'S CALENDAR AT
BrianCain.com/calendar

Made in the USA
Columbia, SC
02 January 2025